BIRD'S EYE VIEW

by
PIFFA SCHRODER
with illustrations by
TIMOTHY JAQUES

GUN ROOM PUBLISHING
LONDON

BIRD'S EYE VIEW

First published in 1995
by Gun Room Publishing
47 Victoria Road, London W8 5RH

A CIP Data record for this book is available from
the British Library

ISBN 1 900284 02 2

Printed and bound by Biddles,
Guildford and King's Lynn

By the same author and published by
Gun Room Publishing:

Banging On
Fair Game

GUN ROOM PUBLISHING
47 Victoria Road, London W8 5RH

For the Maestro
with love

My very grateful thanks to the *Shooting Times,* which first published 'Bear Facts' and 'First Drive'.

I am also deeply indebted to Malcolm Innes, for his inspired renderings of 'MacAlasdair'; to Toby Buchan, for editing and enthusiasm; and, of course, to Tim Jaques, for his patience as much as for his wonderful illustrations.

Contents

Once More Into The Breeches

―――――――――――

It's quite amazing the amount of paraphernalia you have to pack for a shooting trip, wherever it might be. It's not that you have to take more clothes than normal, it's just that all shooting gear seems to take up an inordinate amount of space *per se*. I mean, you can easily pack enough, even including attendant bits and pieces, to see you over a whole week of balls, parties and picnics without any trouble at all. Nothing to it: race meetings or presidential receptions, go-karting or a night at the opera, water-skiing or safaris, desert exploration or high-profile entertainment, rain forests or romance . . . you get the point. Just throw the stuff into a suitcase – not forgetting the cordless curlers or the collar studs, and you could be off anywhere in the world. But shooting seems to demand a ton of luggage all to itself. The only person I have ever met who seems not to need such encumbrances is a tall and charming Scotsman who always appears in a kilt with his gun-slip over his shoulder, a very small bag containing his effects and an enormously long and heavy case holding his bagpipes. He is always perfectly attired for whatever happens to be on the agenda, and only requires to be allowed to play the pipes at every conceivable opportunity during his stay.

What is absolutely fatal is to lay all the stuff out and look at it as you then feel faint and have to go and lie down for a considerable time. My mother, who was a great one for lists, used to make me sit down and write out under different headings (a) everything I could possibly need, (b) everything I had forgotten, followed by a third section of (c) things that might just conceivably come in handy. As – she always remarked darkly – You Never Know. Three pages of foolscap later and I needed a couple of sherpas just to spend the night away. However, to this day I keep an In-Case Case (of which she would undoubtedly have approved) packed and ready and brimming with vital necessities like sterile medical kit, safety pins, fuse-wire, gaffer tape (no really, you can mend a leg or a plane with that stuff), moisturiser, a booklet on what to do if you suddenly find yourself in a tropical forest or in Arctic waters, silk thermals, portable saw, bathplug, gas-filled curling tongs of course, compass, pencil, mascara, mirror for signalling with after you've put on the mascara, arnica, underwater matches, roll of loo paper, earrings, army knife and passport. At a moment's notice, therefore, I am perfectly equipped to go anywhere. Elopement and impulse are on my daily agenda. It's called living in hope if not expectation.

Where were we? Yes: the breeches to start with. Nothing too complicated here – oldest ones for stalking, pristine ones for smart shoots, run-of-the-mill for anything else. For ladies the options are only marginally more interesting – long culottes are possible for foreign shoots and Hampshire, tweed breeks for the rest of the kingdom. (The old Marchioness of Breadalbane went stalking invariably clad in a long tweed skirt and jacket and a flat-topped hat shaped like a large muffin; but then she was on her own ground, and you can wear almost anything you like on your own ground as long as it doesn't frighten the horses.) On really smart shoots in England, or for grouse shooting in Scotland with earls, gentlemen wear shooting suits and take a waterproof jacket in case there's a storm. Pheasant shooting in Scotland, or on most shoots in the south, the only people to wear full shooting suits are stockbrokers and keepers. Gentlemen will wear their favourite old shooting jacket and a pair of (non-matching) tweed breeches.

As far as headgear is concerned, although gentlemen wear correct but very un-sexy tweed caps or – if they are either young enough or old enough – their grandfather's ancient trilby, ladies can wear muffins if they so desire or fur if they are standing by the guns (but definitely not for stalking in) or brown numbers with wide brims, made of proper felt, alive with feathers or shooting brooches all of which makes them look like rather upmarket game-racks.

Jackets are a nightmare for the packer. Tweed, loden, mackintosh or waxed . . . waterproof for winter shoots, but absolutely not if you're going stalking when a Barbour or a loden jacket stands out like a sore thumb on a bleak hillside.

Probably tweed is best all round – although it is permeable unless specially treated, tweed covers most eventualities and you look businesslike and as if you know what you're about. Ladies can, if they are standing with the guns, wear long loden coats lined with fur but if shooting should wear some sort of windproof lined jacket as otherwise you freeze, standing in corners of fields where there is nothing but a prayer between you and Siberia. But then to take every single thing you might need, and to travel with five different sorts of coats and jackets, makes you look as if you've been dispossessed.

There is one drawback. Favourite shooting jackets do invariably, being old and much-loved, carry with them that certain *je ne sais quoi* . . . if you think Calcutta's a bit niffy, try shutting yourself in a car with someone's old Barbour. It's that indefinable mixture of sick and spaniel that's the real bummer. To be fair, I suppose there is only one thing worse: go out stalking for goats in the rutting season, get one, remove the head (you don't even bother gralloching the thing, just bury the carcass, they all do) and, having forgotten to bring a bin-liner, carry the thing back over your shoulders . . . The keeper who did that hung his jacket in a tree for a whole year, right by his house. It kept the roe deer out of the flowerbeds, but even by the end of the twelvemonth it was no better so he burned it, as people just walking past the house used to turn green and make for the bushes.

Smell apart, shooting jackets also have pockets which are full of things which, if you're travelling abroad, you'd really rather they didn't strew about the customs hall when they strip-search you; awful old handkerchiefs, some doubtful bits of kitchen paper, frayed rope (you had to pull a beast down the hill the last time you went stalking, which

presumably accounts for the sorry remains of what had clearly been, in its prime of life, a scrambled-egg bap), a couple of used cartridge cases which have sent all the alarm bells going and is why you're being strip-searched in the first place, a shooting mitten covered in dried gunge and feathers and, before you know where you are, you're being lynched by a large woman in pearls and a Conservative hat. And a couple of those deeply unattractive little yucky things like dessicated sea-slugs, yellow in parts, that you know haven't been in your ears as you now wear proper ear-muffs, but you can't remember either in whose or (it is debatable which is worse) when.

Abroad is a very difficult place to pack for as far as shooting goes and, just to add to the problems, although you can usually borrow a rifle from your host, you always have to take your own shotgun. And airports (or, for that matter, foreign stations of any kind) are not the best places for guns, quite apart from the fact that people tend rather to stare. My husband came back from an extremely smart invitation to shoot snipe in Kashmir only to find, as he disembarked at Heathrow, that his gun-case hadn't made the trip back but had inexplicably got 'left behind' in Srinagar. (*Srinagar*, for God's sake – you could just imagine them out there, sitting round in the hangar that evening rubbing their hands over the day's haul: 'Goody goody gumdrops, oh my word, ooh a pair too, ooooh goodness.') Needless to say, he never saw them again.

MORAL: remember not only to take all relevant Shotgun and Firearms Certificates when travelling abroad, but also to insure everything up to the hilt . . .

Then there are the sticks and the shooting seats, the cartridge bags and belts, the gun- or rifle-slips, the hip flask and the dreaded ear-muffs; the scarves, house presents, gloves, handwarmers, binoculars, the extra socks, the cartridges or rifle ammunition and of course, that purgatory for the perfectionist packer, the boots.

Footwear takes up a disproportionately huge amount of space. The choice is large enough: wellington boots (although not if you're a gentleman – gentlemen only wear leather on their feet, not on grounds of comfort but because of what their grandfathers said about people who wore gumboots), sturdy ankle-boots (climbing variety), leather knee-boots (Spanish shooting variety), old army numbers, or those nice broguey things with leather fringes (but only if it's for the grouse butts, or you're female). Most people's shooting or stalking boots look as though they've been brought up from the *Mary Rose*, although I remember an Austrian who came to stay in Scotland who, for some reason, took inordinate pride in his boots which, on the first day out anyway, did look as if a soldier-servant had spent the best part of a week bulling them beforehand. Every night the Austrian, a man of meticulous habit and absolutely no idea of Scottish shooting lodges, would leave his boots outside his bedroom door, obviously expecting that someone would clean them for him. As we didn't have any soldier-servants in the house, and I certainly wasn't going to spend the nights spitting, polishing or warming teaspoons over them, the boots stayed out where he put them. Every morning he would come out of his room, collect them with a loud sigh and (I discovered later) buff them up on the lining of the curtains.

One evening, we all decided to get up the next day before dawn and go goose flighting. During the evening, and all through the night, there was the most stupendous storm. Unfortunately the house was not what you might term totally waterproof: the roof leaked like a sieve, you had to put towels under the windowsills and buckets had to be strewn everywhere along passages so that, under meteorological conditions such as this, corridor-creeping was not advisable. By the time I rose at 4.30, water had poured in everywhere and was running down the walls like Victoria Falls. Having checked to see that everyone was awake, I knocked on the Austrian's door having also brought him, in my best Sister of Charity mode, a mug of early morning tea (he was never at his best until lunchtime anyway), at which point I discovered that the carpet outside his room was like a quagmire, thanks to a stream of water cascading off the top of the door frame. However, as there was nothing I could do about it right then, I went on downstairs to the kitchen and set about making toast and coffee for the other members of the party who were already on their way down, dressed but muted.

We sat quietly round the table as one does at that sort of hour, not saying much, trying to focus and not crunch the toast, listening to the creaking floorboards above which indicated that the Austrian, although probably not in very good shape, was at least alive. Then we heard his door open. There was a moment of silence followed by an explosion, a roar of unutterable fury. 'GOTT IN HIMMEL' the Austrian bellowed, 'DAS IST . . .' (his voice went up several octaves) 'AAAAAARGH . . .' Then the door slammed, the house reverberated, and there was silence again.

We all looked at each other in stunned amazement. 'What on earth . . . do you think . . . I wonder if . . . perhaps you'd better go up and see . . . no *you* go, he's *your* guest,' so I went.

It transpired that he had gone out to retrieve his boots as usual, had clambered into them with his eyes half shut and had suddenly found himself up to his ankles in cold water. The funniest part about it was he that thought that one of us had done it, on purpose, to bait him, and he didn't find it in the least amusing.

And he didn't get a goose that morning, either.

High Cockalorum

<hr />

Iknew it was a mistake the minute I'd put the phone down. Having not touched a shotgun for over a dozen years, here I was accepting an invitation to shoot. They were so persuasive, so totally unfussed: 'NO problem, you can borrow the 20-bore – last day of the season – very relaxed, promise – sorry it's so last-minute but the head man now says the boys can't get off school that weekend – oh nothing to worry about there, it's like riding a bicycle you never forget anyway it'll be FUN – you'll know everyone you will come won't you that's smashing . . .'

I love last-minute invitations, they're much more exciting and I hate planning months in advance – you never know, you might be dead by then and you'd be so cross at what you'd missed – so that didn't bother me. So it only left six days which were due to be filled by being in Scotland busy with the end of the hind quota, then straight down south for the weekend shoot . . . jet-set stuff, this sporting life. Six days left no time for nerves; it also left no time for any shooting practice. BIG mistake.

Shooting with a shotgun is rather like making love: the more you do it the better you get and the more fun it is. Ability and enjoyment are the result of assiduous practice. Unlike with a rifle where you either have, for some miraculous reason, an 'eye' for it or you don't – and too much practice can easily get you stale – with a shotgun practice is everything. One of the reasons I'd originally given up shooting was quite simply that I never got enough practice. I shot perhaps five days a year at home and always at the end of the line where, if I was lucky, three birds might come over during the day. And because I was therefore not even a moderately good shot I would never have dreamed of shooting 'away' where, as a woman, you were looked on and watched as if you had the pox. Added to which, I suffered from the sort of exam nerves which entailed having to hurry off before every first drive behind a bush. As much for the sake of the environment as for my own peace of mind, therefore, I stopped shooting and could then concentrate on enjoying the shoot.

'Don't be silly, you love it, of course you shoot,' people would cry – which is daft – like saying that because you like caviare you should be master of a trawler in the Caspian. (Or skiing: once you've renounced the humiliation of spending most of your time face down in the snow snivelling at exasperated *moniteurs* while other people whizz past yelling merrily, skiing holidays actually become fun. I just hate doing things badly. I don't ski now, either.)

I arrived as bidden on the Friday evening. Lovely house party of all ages and all friends, cosy and relaxed, and the fires blazing while a good January storm lashed outside. According to the forecast, a severe drop in temperature and snow imminent. Having spent the drive down sick with fear and bitterly regretting this enticing lure to come and shoot, I went to bed praying for tornadoes.

Saturday morning dawned. I'd spend one of those amazing nights of total panic where you wake up every 17 minutes convinced that the clock has stopped so that by 7.30 when you finally get up you've got bags the size of cabin trunks under the eyes and have to wear dark glasses for breakfast. This looks particularly stupid in winter. As predicted, of course, the storm had gone through and there had been a very hard-freezing frost. No mist (a white-out would have been nice) but bright and very cold, crisp and clear. By 9 o'clock everyone was gathering outside chomping for the off in cheerful pandemonium. Dogs, released from kennels and cars, met each other, hackles up, then tore about galvanised by shouting and the cold. The young, all wearing silly hats and muffled up to the eyeballs, were being hugely unhelpful and our host, trying to maintain a semblance of calm, was trying to install order. 'Now Soph, you've got Dickie's sixteen-bore, right? And Jack and William have got twelves and – yes do, of course he wouldn't mind, anyone else need a belt? Right, ah, here come the gallant neighbours, morning everyone, now where was I? YES: everyone got the right cartridges? Owen, just the man, check them, will you, Harriet's walked off with my bag – NO not THERE, geddorfthat, BLOODY animal always does it right there on the doorstep, typical – morning Arthur, well done, and Jill that's great, over there if you can next to the Land-Rover, somebody watch those bottles CHRIST who let the puppies out . . . '

The rest of the house party crunches out into the bedlam, chatting and greeting and laughing, booted and furred; daughters with boyfriends lark about, more cars arrive; beaters congregate, huffing ghosts in the yard, their bow-legged springers marking time impatiently from foot to foot and a small terrier, quietly intent on his own affairs, looks round shiftily and, squatting, neatly evacuates his bowels into an open cartridge bag on the gravel. I want to crawl into an outhouse and pretend I'd got lost. 'RIGHT then, er, anyone under twenty-five onto the tractor, WATCH THE . . . oh well, it had a dent in it anyway . . . everyone else follow Owen, yes Simon, can you take the Humphrieses with you, Harriet darling you go in the Volvo and I'll take whoever's left and the bottles, come on dogs, OK let's GO'.

The first drive was brilliant – woodcock flitting about, dogs skidding over thick ice on the pond, some lovely fast cackling birds, bright sunshine, lots of barracking and video cameras, everyone in high form, the most perfect morning. I didn't hit a thing.

The next drive was even better; tall woods on the side of

a vertical hill, ponies galloping furiously round a field below, pheasants like starlings, some spectacular hat-doffing shots, the whole of the valley spread out behind us, sheep and smoke from small cottages in the distance. And I didn't hit a thing.

Two more drives before the Bullshot and the King's Ginger. Sophie had got her first pheasant, the young men were brilliant, the old hands stood behind and shouted Well Done, the pale midday sun was warming for the last drive before lunch. And I still hadn't hit a thing.

Some two hours later, fortified by some tremendously good osso bucco followed by a really therapeutic steamed pud (I didn't dare drink anything but they were all into the beer, and port with the celery and Stilton), I took out my gun again with feverish determination, for the one last drive of the day. This was going to be it. I knew it. We'd all filled out a scrap of paper with our bets at lunch as to what the final score was going to be, our host had added a dozen more onto what I'd written down because, he said, this was going to be my drive, I'd see how easy it was, all those ridiculous nerves before lunch, just give them four times the amount of lead you think you need as they're going like dingbats, no problem, and he raised his glass and toasted me for luck. I laughed modestly (not too difficult, under the circumstances) and toasted them all back, and wagered that I'd probably be, ha ha, the only person who'd ever come to shoot and not hit a thing. Much laughter at that, they were all willing me on, all I had to do was go for it.

That last drive was magic. Standing down by the river in a huge deep valley way below the house, and the birds were as tall as steeples. It was the time for the old and experienced shots and we watched and cheered and it was perfect and then a couple of the boys connected and then everyone else got into the swing of it and the birds kept on coming higher and higher from the great dark woods behind the house. And as the light started to fade the snow came, gently at first then in thick soft drifts, filling the evergreens with cold blossom, muffling the river banks and shawling round the trunks of trees. You could see the flame of each shot before you heard its noise. And finally the whistle was blown, and the dogs and the pickers-up took over, and the guns left their pegs and joined up and began walking back up the long hill in the white gloaming, the slow, contented walk of a well-tested party on their way home after the last day of the season, congratulating the host, the keeper, the beaters and each other on a truly wonderful day in which, I knew, I hadn't hit a thing.

A huge tea waiting when we got back to the house, then everyone who had to leave left, and the rest of us went off tobogganing (it was really thick on the ground by then) or sank into baths, or slept. And in the evening after dinner there were cards, and champagne, and mad mess-games involving men standing on bottles wielding broomsticks;

and talk, far into the night. My earlier incompetence was summarily dismissed. 'You'll just have to come back next season, right? You'll show us all up with what you'll have learned at the shooting school – promise? – no stopping you then – meanwhile what is MUCH more important is that your glass is empty, hang on a sec. . . .' They were fantastic.

The following day, the party split up shortly after lunch as everyone reckoned that the heavy snowfalls and the likelihood of thick fog didn't bode well for motorway journeys home. There was the usual disorganised flap that accompanies every end-of-party departure: chaos in the boot room, men lugging suitcases downstairs complaining of women's packing, dogs getting underfoot. The cat had been discovered locked into the larder and happily ensconced in the remains of the kedgeree, we were all feeling wonderfully well, very spoiled and extremely loath to leave.

Finally, everything packed up in the cars, hugs and kisses all round, lots of 'safe journey' and 'see you soon' and 'bye darling', and the family stood and waved madly as we all climbed into our respective vehicles and revved up. It was like the start of Le Mans. Backing smartly away, I swung the steering wheel round in what I hoped was a professional and nonchalant manner with one hand, and waved merrily out of the window with the other. The car skidded, there was a small interval (which you could have measured in microseconds) followed by the most ghastly crunching noise and everything came to a swift halt. The car was suddenly 6 inches shorter. With unerring accuracy, I'd backed slap into the corner of the barn.

It was, of course, the only thing I'd managed to hit all weekend.

Game Birds

T here used to be 'ladies who lunch'. Now there are 'ladies who shoot'. There is a growing mafia of them, a gleefully emancipated band of females unlikely to chain themselves to the gun cabinets but nevertheless, to the consternation evident in some of the gentlemen's clubs, deemed to be a force to be reckoned with. In these uncertain days, as we lurch unsurely towards the millennium, it has become an accepted (if not a universally acknowledged) fact that there are, indeed, ladies who can shoot.

But the problem for a lady shot remains the same as it has always been: unless you are lucky enough to enjoy, through inheritance or marriage, land on which it is a perfectly undisputed fact that you may and do carry a gun, then it is an uphill struggle. You may fire away until you drop at shooting schools. You can hint or cajole, whinge or plead but, until someone actually asks you out to shoot in the field, there is no way of getting on to a shoot. And no gentleman – for whom and by whom shooting is run – will ever ask an unknown quantity for a day's shooting especially if it happens to be female. His peers, not to mention his keeper, will all (or so the thinking goes) express their disapproval unequivocally. And no syndicate worth its salt (or anxious to retain its members) would ever accept an unknown female gun if none of the members can vouch for her safety or ability. It may be understandable from the male standpoint but it is utterly depressing from the bird's-eye view.

I was extremely fortunate in that my first invitation to shoot came out of the blue when, as explained earlier, I hadn't even picked up a gun for a dozen years, had totally forgotten how to do it and then proceeded to do it extremely badly. However, fired (as it were) with a mixture of humiliation and determination, I hurried back from the débâcle of that day and immediately booked in for what seemed to be a lifetime of lessons, as there is nothing worse than doing things badly, especially those things that you want to do really well. (It is even worse when you have been seen to do them badly in public). So I went at the clays with a vengeance.

Now it's all very well for men to sneer at 'those damned women cluttering up the shooting schools' – they've all been at the sport since the age of seven when they had to undergo the ritual small boys' induction to shooting: a year with a pop-gun carried under the arm (corks to be removed when climbing a fence); then a year carrying a .410, empty, practising the swing; at last, aged nine, being allowed to fire a live cartridge, followed by a year of practice at thrown cans, clays and so forth before; aged ten, being awarded the hard-earned accolade – a box of cartridges and an invitation to stand, under strict supervision, at their first drive. Men who shoot well shoot very well indeed – like potty training, it can all be ascribed to early and stern indoctrination. By and large, however, insofar as etiquette in the shooting field is concerned, girls are not encouraged in the same fashion.

So there is a lot to make up in terms of time, experience and expertise. And of course the more you slog away at your shooting lessons, the more difficult you realise it is and, also, the more there is to learn. And although you're getting better, you feel you're getting nowhere and that you will never be able to do the thing properly at all. For there is (as every gentleman will tell you and – be it never forgotten – they are The

Experts) a world of difference between learning to shoot at moving objects, which any fool can do after a while (after all, as they say, 'He that shoots oft shall at last hit the mark'), and its becoming second nature – a reflex action that enables you to fire every shot without having to think, each time, of lead, swing, distance, etc. And it is this part that takes, possibly, a lifetime to achieve.

Then a girlfriend, who knew of my endeavours, invited me to stay and shoot on her Ladies' Day. It was the bravest, the most generous, thing she can ever have done.

I turned up, as before, in a lather of nerves. After all, a lady, if she is to be invited out into the shooting field, must shoot at least as well as, if not better than, the men who will all be carefully observing her and noting down (for later discussion amongst themselves) any little point, any small digression from the supremely high standard set by Gentleman Shots. She must be able to handle a gun with confidence and ease, and at the same time be modest and correct; she must therefore not only be a supremely safe and good shot, with charm and preferably a modicum of good looks (not too many, men distrust 'glamour' on the shooting field), but must also possess enough guile to make it clear that, however competent she may be, she Knows Her Place. (Actually if she shot even half as badly as half the men on half the shoots in the kingdom, she would probably not be allowed out in the first place. That is Lady's Law.) Even given the fact that this was going to be a Ladies' Day, to me, a novice, it promised to be totally terrifying.

It wasn't. It was early December, we were far enough north for it to be biting cold, the evening sky as I arrived was cloudless and streaked with lavender. The house was deliciously warm and pretty, there were flowers everywhere, drinks before a deep hot bath with lashings of Floris, and a cosy dinner so that I might get to know the other girls who all (it really is a mafia) knew each other and had shot together for years. The only man around was our hostess's husband. There would be some other men who would join us for dinner the following evening after the shoot, but otherwise it was girls only. Our host pronounced himself enchanted with his harem and was assuming the role of butler, chauffeur, general gofer, cartridge carrier, photographer in the field, etc., and afterwards, cleaner of boots. He would not, of course, be shooting.

The whole atmosphere of a Ladies' Day is totally different from that of an ordinary shooting day. It starts at breakfast. Women are much more *civilised* at breakfast than men. There is no groaning sideboard (full of cholesterol and very *bloating*) but one huge creamy dish of scrambled eggs with some very crisp bacon plus mueslis, lots of fruit, croissants, freshly baked bread and oatcakes, delicious marmalades and various types of honey, and different teas and steaming coffee. Everyone has come down in good time, as women don't like to *rush*. All the papers lie around but, apart from checking up on the odd scandal and the star signs, everyone is too busy gossiping to read. Long discussions about the weather forecast and the right clothing. 'Well, what about that lovely furry thing, that would look great with those culottes, wouldn't it, then you can always take it off if it gets too warm, but thermals definitely, the east side of those woods is arctic . . . Morning darling, sleep well? Gosh what a divine colour, you look wonderful, isn't cashmere just the best . . .' We chatter on. The host, in butler mode, is replenishing coffee cups; he has obviously got everything under complete control and only demands that his wife enjoy her day. 'No I've done that, relax, don't worry about a thing. Soup and drinks in the car, Mrs Mole says lunch is all organised, your flask is filled and I've put it beside your gun . . .'

About 8.30 everyone filters upstairs and there's more laughter and chat through open doors. Down again, fifteen minutes to go and no panicking. The keeper is waiting in the gun room. 'Morning Billy, everything OK? Now just let me introduce you . . . ' Everyone clambering into boots, checking and comparing notes. 'Hey what a marvellous hat, and *golly* that's clever, let's see – right, it just zips in and out. I say, can I copy that? It's brilliant . . .' The keeper grinning and chatting up the guests, saying he's got more beaters and pickers-up than usual today as half the county has turned up to see the ladies shooting. We crunch out into the yard where the beaters are three deep and nudging each other. The cars have been loaded up, everyone has their guns, the hostess is still looking after details. 'Everyone warm enough? No, there's masses of time, nip up and get another one . . . Cartridges? loads of them in the van if you run out *which* reminds me where's my belt? . . . now come on the photographer, got to have a record of the girls' team for the book – right Billy, shall we go?' and we all pile into the vehicles feeling well and happy and relaxed and the day goes like a dream and, miracle of miracles, I don't totally disgrace myself.

Compare this to an ordinary day's shooting party. Here, breakfast kicks off with the men, all wearing highly coloured shooting stockings with *fright*fully amusing things written on the turnover bits like Come Here/Bloody Dog or Bugger/Lloyds, all equally determined to prove to each other their own general machismo, sitting behind the serious papers grunting things like 'Yers . . . market looks a bit sleepy, doesn't it?' and 'See old Fotheringham-flyte Stuart's snuffed it, silly old fart' and helping themselves to yet another plateful from the sideboard where the kippers, sausages, fried eggs, black pudding and kedgeree stand in wait like the dogs salivating below. (There was one house where I remember there were sixteen separate chafing dishes for breakfast, and that didn't include the tureen of porridge.) The women have been relegated down to one end of the table where they sit quietly making small (very small – men don't like *chatter* at breakfast) talk, and wondering guiltily how they can get away and go antique hunting in the afternoon. Silence is punctuated by noises of toast and the occasional aside.

Then the host flings down his newspaper, scattering crumbs and cutlery and upending the odd cup, pushes back his chair and, leaping up, announces loudly 'GOD-is-that-the-time-right-meet-in-five-minutes-outside-the-back-

door. Better be smartish about it too, old Jack'll have a seizure if we don't start by nine prompt – Janey, JANEY' (yelling through the kitchen door where the hostess has been seen making her escape) 'you'll see the girls are all right will you and lock the dogs in and have you sorted out a proper lunch I want decent claret for God's sake not that awful tenants' rotgut and have you arranged to go and pick up Jake from the station someone's got to do it why do I have to think of everything we must go men's work and all that see you later huh?'

The male guests are in a turmoil, not having allowed enough time for everything, summoning boots, wives, missing clothing. 'DON'T say you moved them off the fridge. I SPECIFICALLY put them there so I'd know where they were and where the DEVIL are they now I can't possibly manage without proper gloves for God's sake so go and look in the car NOW I don't know for crying out loud just go and LOOK of course it's raining you stupid woman what the HELL do you expect no you haven't time for that now just MOVE.'

Keepers and underlings stand quietly by the back door talking in undertones and watching, the host is still roaring – something about seeing the fires are properly laid and going by the time they get back – some of the more stalwart wives are waiting and ready outside, there are still eight men in the back hall all in a lather and garotting themselves with long scarves and bits of towelling, getting under one another's feet, standing on the dogs, picking up each other's guns, struggling into the wrong Barbours and swearing. finally the door slams; there's the noise of cars revving up and squealing tyres and off they go, braying. The house seems to sigh, and there is silence at last.

In the old days in America, in the Deep South, young girls were brought up on the dictum 'Pretty if you can, pleasant if it kills you'. But then, on Ladies' Days, you don't even have to try.

First Drive

There are a few bits of information which, in a truly perfect world, should be programmed into the genetic system, thus enabling the newborn babe to spring, like Athene, fully armed and prepared for all eventualities from its mother's womb. The sort of small, unimportant things that make all the difference between a good and a bad day. Like how to get into a carton of milk, how to ensure you don't get left with a bung of cement at the top of the toothpaste tube, what to do with 5p pieces without making your eyes water, and how to tell from a map the length of time a journey will take.

It's not that women can't map-read, of course. Certainly not. On the contrary, we are brilliant at it. Athene could have done it with her helmet on. It's just that we calculate distances differently to men – a different set of priorities perhaps. We want to be able to get wherever we're going peacefully, easily, with our hair intact and the occasional diversion for the odd necessities of life without *hassle*. Men, who learn how to map-read by driving tanks in the army, don't understand this sort of thinking; they sigh incredulously and then take you through it step by painful step. 'Now look here,' they say, speaking slowly, as if trying to explain to an orang-utan how to peel a banana, 'let me show you. It's all a matter of planning your co-ordinates. ETA equals ETD, right? You just measure out the distance *there*, then you look up the mileage converter key at the front *there* so you know how many miles there are to the centimetre . . . What? oh you prefer inches do you? ha ha, typical woman . . . then you multiply by fifty-one which is your average speed isn't it? – well it is, you can take it from me – and Bob's your uncle. Absolute doddle.' Not from where I'm standing, squire.

The first time I was ever invited to shoot on a syndicate day, the route-planning figured heavily. My husband had joined the syndicate halfway through the previous season and had only shot with them a couple of times, on neither of which occasions had I been able to be with him. So I didn't know any of the other members, and had never been to the shoot. This particular weekend, he was suddenly required to fly off abroad for some hastily convened meeting, so he rang the syndicate organiser to make his apologies for the following day when he was meant to be shooting. He then asked if – since it was such a last-minute cancellation – it would help if I came in his place. Well, er, yes, they said, it *was* a trifle irregular of course but, seeing as it was probably now too late to get anyone else, um, why not . . . Is she, um, does she, er, well not to put too fine a point on it can she actually, er, *shoot*? 'No problem' he cried airily, 'hasn't shot an awful lot but perfectly SAFE you know, just keep an eye on her, she'll be fine,' then he put the phone down, very pleased with himself, told me what he'd arranged, threw some clothes into a case, waved goodbye and left for the office.

This was Friday morning. I spent the day in a frenzy. It was actually a pretty foolhardy thing for him to have done – I really hadn't shot all that much and then mostly with friends who never seemed to mind what you missed and were enthusiastic, understanding and very kind. I'd never been out alone with a bunch of strange men – not in a shooting field, at any rate. The whole of Friday was spent checking I'd got everything I was meant to have, taking the gun in and out of the safe half a dozen times to make sure all the bits were in the right places, making little piles of things by the front door so I wouldn't leave anything behind the next morning – boots, ear-muffs, cartridge bag, cartridges, gun-slip, shooting gloves, jacket, shooting hat, plasters In Case, handbag and money – it seemed endless – all ready to pack into the car. And I suddenly realised I

didn't have a clue as to where I was meant to be going, who the organiser was, or the head keeper – nothing. So, praying that he hadn't already left, I rang my husband at the office.

Mistake. Men don't *like* being rung at the office, so I got the 'I-will-say-this-only-once' routine. 'Good heavens woman, look it up on the map for God's sake, yes, same name as the village, couldn't be easier – no, forty minutes door to door, through the village, two miles on there's a white farmhouse on the left, you'll see all the cars parked by a signpost, be there nine-ish, must-rush-now-see-you-Sunday.'

I got out the map and the Rescue Remedy. At least I now had the name of the place, and I'd managed to get the phone number. If he'd said forty minutes, that was because he knew the way, had been there before, and anyhow always drove like Jehu. The weather forecast didn't sound that cheerful, so I'd have to allow for that too. So: add on another half-hour for bad weather, getting lost, floods on road, trees struck by lightning (you know the sort of things that happen to you when you're pushed). Add another ten minutes just in case – breakdown, petrol leak, enlisting good-looking local for help, finding garage, pub etc. Total eighty minutes. Reckon on a further ten minutes to pack the car (remembering to take shotgun out of safe and Shotgun Certificate in case stopped by constabulary) and double-check everything, and the journey was going to take me one and a half hours.

The trouble with time is that it's so unpredictable. You go to a Wagner opera for instance, sit quietly for four hours, then look at your watch and realise that only twenty minutes have elapsed. On the other hand you can put your feet up to listen to the 1 o'clock news and all at once it's mid-afternoon, the dog is whimpering by the front door with its legs crossed, the Magimix is all over the kitchen ceiling, the phone (which you'd taken off the hook so as to listen to the news uninterrupted) has that patient-Griselda voice repeating 'Please replace the handset and try again later', and the police car is outside with the blue lights flashing.

As far as journeys are concerned, I don't trust time. I hate being late and I've always had train fever. I hate travelling with people who favour the last-on-first-off principle. I hate having to scamper through the airport corridors lugging the Duty Free, struggling against the jet-lagged incoming hordes while the voice over the intercom pleads 'Flight FU Two to Bulawayo, will Mrs Schroder, last remaining passenger, come IMMEDIATELY to gate one-oh-niner where the flight is now closing' and you're busting a gut to keep on going and the plane seems to have been parked out at Datchet and you can't utter as you've got your boarding ticket clamped between your teeth and all you want to do is sit down and sob . . .

But I digress. Suffice to say that if I'm told forty minutes, then to allow an hour and a half doesn't strike me, personally, as unreasonable. Over-anxious perhaps, but better safe than sorry. Especially for a shoot. Especially when it's your first appearance amongst a whole lot of strangers, and even more especially when you're a woman. You know they'll all be watching, you know the first bird in the first drive is inevitably going to come over you, and you know, you just KNOW you're going to miss it and they will all see and it will be ghastly and humiliating and why in the name of all that's holy did you ever agree to do it? . . .

Saturday dawned. I got up, gulped coffee, dressed and rushed round like a mad thing, packed the car, remembered the gun and was on the road at 7.29 as planned. Maps on the passenger seat, mobile phone and contact number at the ready, route instructions written out, torch and spade in the boot in case of snowdrifts, apple for breakfast-in-transit in the glove-box. Organisation Grade A. No traffic to speak of, an hour and a half should do it comfortably, no need to put the foot down, just follow the route plan and stop twitching.

As it turned out, I need not have panicked so much. The shoot itself was fantastic, the first drive (which went according to prognosis) went fine and a couple of birds dashed themselves into the shot pattern, everyone was sweet and kind and cheerful and funny, a delicious lunch at the local pub, the head keeper a star ('Tell you what mum, you're walking gun this drive, why don't you just stand in there, that's where they always come back in this wind, you got some corkers back there just now, mind yourself on that wire'), my guardian angel was in overdrive and they all could not have been less frightening or more generous. I admitted the previous day's crippling nerves and they all laughed and made nice noises.

What I did not own up to (nor did I confess to my husband later) was the length of time that, in my panic, I'd allowed for the journey. I'd been told forty minutes. Forty minutes on the dot after setting off, I'd found myself by the white farmhouse. However, as it was then only nine minutes past eight there wasn't a soul around, except for a tractor driver who looked at me strangely as he clattered past. I drove back into the village where (it being Saturday) nothing was happening; I bought a yoghurt off a dairy float, found the pub car park and, having eaten the yoghurt and my apple, curled up in the back of the car and slept fitfully until 8.55. I then drove back to the white farmhouse, where the only vehicles around belonged to the keeper and the senior picker-up – he of the tractor. He commiserated, told me the other guns weren't due to arrive for another twenty minutes, and said that if only I'd made myself known to him before I could have gone and had coffee with his missus.

Next time I drove to a shoot, I thought, I'd bring a thermos in the car as well.

Weasel Words

W hen I was at school we spent a whole term on English Language and the parsing thereof, and I first came across the term 'composite word'. The German language is full of composite words – *Obergruppenführer*, for instance – and a word which basically means 'porter' is composed of several words which separately mean something like 'senior covered in gold braid master train corridor carrier in charge', or somesuch. And that famous Welsh village, the name of which is a conglomerate of words telling you how to get there, what it looks like, and for all I know how many pubs it has, is a good example.

A really glorious composite word is an Eskimo one which reads '*aulisautisarsiniarpungar*' (accent on the 'pung') which means 'I wish I had a bit of string to use as a fishing line'. And for those interested in the etymological development of our own dear native tongue, the Australian word for foreplay, according to Informed Sources, is 'briceyerselfsheila'.

The English language is full of the most terrible minefields and pitfalls, and sporting language is no less so. Spare a thought for those poor visitors to have to master the thing. Why should 'covert' mean either 'a shelter, especially a thicket, hiding game' ('game' is difficult enough anyway if you're a foreigner) or, when followed by the word 'coat', mean 'a short light overcoat usually with a velvet collar'? Why a 'towered bird'? I know now, because I looked it up, that it means a bird that soars up vertically after being shot, before plummeting to earth from a great height – but originally I'd imagined that people were talking about a tired bird (you know those sorts of accents where they say 'hice' instead of 'house') and felt rather sorry for it. Then you get Scottish foresters muttering about the 'ruddy damndrons', which is perfectly logical if you're a Scottish forester but incomprehensible even to most Sassenachs, let alone a Spaniard or a Swede. Now that we're all part of the great European Community we really should try and make life easier for our Continental friends. Mind you, I once heard some Belgians discussing one of Britain's more senior politician's acumen and ability and general grasp of Common Market issues and, to the comment *'Mais il raisonne bien, tout de même'*, came the reply *'Mon cher, il résonne comme un tambour'*.

However, *revenons* (as they say over there) *à nos moutons*. Imagine that you have invited a group of visitors from abroad to shoot, all of whom are particularly anxious to do the thing correctly and *à l'anglaise*. They have all gone to the trouble of visiting one or two of the well-known London shooting shops to get kitted up properly beforehand, and thus give the impression of having stepped straight out of a catalogue, as everything is clearly new and uncreased. Some will have 'proper' English shotguns, some will not. 'Moy wurrd' says Spasm, the ninety-eight-year old head keeper who, although almost totally deaf, hears the rustle of folded money through an eight-foot thick wall and says things like 'Dukes and earls with me, the rest of the guns with the bea'ers' when he doesn't like the look of a day's party; 'moy wurrd, arrr well, one of 'em Aya things arrr you'll 'ave to moind when you open that surr, they don't 'arf get buggered up with gunge them spanny things an' oi'm not going to spend 'arf the noit cleanin' the bloody 'stractors off of 'em.' And you see the panic-stricken miens of the visitors, most of whom have never been further north than London W.1., trying to grapple with the idiom of this wasteland into which they have been transported (in this case, a fine day's partridge shooting in Suffolk) and saying to each other in fevered undertones *'Qu'est-ce qu'il fabrique là le bonhomme, t'as compris quelquechose? moi non'*, or – shades of Manuel – faces screwed up in demented shell-shocked incomprehension and a chorus of *'¿QUE?'*

Mind you, you don't have to be foreign to be rendered totally boss-eyed by the local vernacular. Farmers' shoots are probably the most difficult as half the time you haven't an iota what they're on about anyway. 'Hmmmm,' some old boy grunts as you're trudging through the leaves into a tall wood, 'narsty bit o' epicormic growth there, old Arthur'd better do summat about tha' . . . ' and you wonder if anyone's called the doctor but there doesn't seem to be any panic. Or bouncing along (you're on as walking gun next drive) in, say, Lincolnshire, and the world of *Fowler's Modern English Usage* takes on a whole new meaning. They're all munching things that look like sheep's gonads which turn out to be sodden pork pies, so enunciation isn't helped. '. . . An' the ould cow she 'ad the staaagerrs an' oi arsed Bob wot 'e did when 'is cow 'ad it a year or sos back an 'e said parafeeen, so oi gives 'er parafeeen an' she goes an' dois. An' oi arsed 'im la'er wot 'appened with 'is cow when 'e give her the parafeeen seein' as moine doied, an' 'e jus' says foony tha', moine doied tew . . . '

It's not just the regional dialect that is difficult either, it's the buzzwords. It took me a full twenty minutes, standing in a nice warm spinney waiting for woodcock, to separate two different conversations going on sotto voce behind me – one of which concerned the excellence of the earthworms ('bluddy crackers they be') produced by the sycamore humus on which the woodcock were due to come in and feed, and the other which involved the relative merits of treble bob majors versus grandsire majors – until I worked out that the local farmers who were acting as pickers-up were also part of the village bell-ringing team.

Then there are those little things which, certainly to a foreigner, could be a bit puzzling. It's not that your guests are mentally challenged, it's just that they're not *British*. The difference, say, between the terms 'game bag' and 'old bag' (one being leather and canvas, the other leathery and female) has thrown many a good man. Or something like 'tall birds' – an expression which has been known to send Frenchmen, more used to reading *Vogue* than the *Shooting Times*, into a lather of expectation. The term 'rough shoot' should be used carefully, too, if amongst the guests you have one who has arrived carrying his effects in a handbag. Even terminology like 'cocks' and 'hens' sometimes needs explaining, especially if the day has started off in a farmyard: I heard an Italian once in a state of high dudgeon because, he said, he thought he'd been invited to shoot pheasants. And then of course it is vital to spell out very carefully what is on the proscribed list for the day (on the Continent they shoot anything that moves) – we had quite a difficult time trying to placate the keeper's small daughter after one foreign gun announced that he'd shot a 'leetle furry ting' which turned out to be a hamster, about which he was inordinately pleased.

Another point that is worth bringing up with a party of foreigners is the matter of what might be termed, in *Almanach de Gotha* circles, 'unseemly language'. It is vital to explain to people from abroad (or indeed to any innocent visitor, come to think of it) that, north of the border, swearing is in NO way disrespectful or vulgar, and merely adds weight, emphasis or gravitas to the subject under discussion. Thus 'a bloody great dram', or 'the sodding rain' – or even the West Coast 'whazzafucksamattamon' (usually addressed to a gun who has failed to connect with anything during a drive) – are perfectly acceptable speech terms. Under no circumstances, however, should the words be individually pronounced.

When I was a child we had a lovely and gentle Scottish gardener whose efforts in the flowerbeds were always being thwarted by the local fauna. One day he arrived at the door in tears, holding the remains of a small shredded shrub, and confronted my mother. When suffering from any extremes of emotion he invariably fell into an awful long-winded stammer, which meant you knew what he was about to say a good few seconds before he could actually say it. My mother was a dab hand at this, and totally unfazeable. 'See this mum, what a b- b- b- b- b- . . .' 'I know, it *is* a shame, isn't it?' 'Must have been one of yon f- f- f- f- f- . . .' 'Yes you're right Duncan, probably *was* a rabbit'.

Down the Line

---

*The sort of remarks that a lady shot
may expect to hear in the field.*

These fall in to three categories:

1) *Conciliatory, expert-to-beginner*

'Jolly tricky in this wind aren't they?'
'No, I think the birds are coming *this* way'
'Dear lady, can I suggest . . .?'
'No I'm sure *one* came down'
'Curling a bit, you know'
'Ah yes, a favourite shot of the old King's, as I recall'

2) *Double-edged sword*

'Heavens, a lady shooting, well well'
'I say, are you all right? Jolly nasty bruise that'
'No don't worry, I wasn't even going to try for it'
'Bless my soul, never seen *that* done before'
'Shoot quite a bit with a rifle do you?'
'Have you ever tried keeping both eyes open?'

3) *Brutally frank and honest*

'WELL, wouldn't like to have to eat THAT one . . . '
'Dammit woman, don't just stand there and *wave* the thing'
'This really isn't an officer's shoot any more, is it?'
'Why don't you shoot where it's going rather than where it's
    been?'
'Well at least she wasn't on the next peg, thank God'

The Alternative Shoot

The days of the huge Edwardian shoots have gone for ever, or so I read in a newspaper article. And about time too. There is something almost indecent nowadays about those lines and lines of dead birds, laid out in serried ranks, and about the record bags for which our forebears competed. As present thinking turns, quite rightly, to the idea of conservation of game and of the countryside, so more and more people are thinking in terms of wild game rather than reared, and even those may not last long. But this does not mean that shooting should stop as, of course, without it there wouldn't be any wild game at all. Conservation means management and management means control – shooting, in this case – which in turn means someone doing it. And there is nothing to decree that you shouldn't enjoy doing it: anyone who thinks otherwise is no better than the Puritans who disapproved of bear-baiting not because it gave pain to the bear but because it gave pleasure to the spectators. That it was barbaric didn't enter the equation.

I kept a cutting from the *Herald Tribune*, dated the 2nd. of October (I think it was some time in the late 60s) which reads: 'The *préfet* of Paris explained today why he had declared the hunting season open in the city, where game is to be found only on the table and may be attacked only with a knife and fork. It was, he said, to preserve the right of urbanites to dream. "It is well known", he wrote, "that the pleasure of hunting is quite distinct from other sports." The *préfet* did not want to deprive Parisians of that portion of dream so essential to urban civilisation.'

An inordinate amount of very simple pleasure can be given to the spectator at something totally uncontroversial like a clay pigeon or skeet shoot. They are both the most infuriating and (if well laid-out) the most testing of sports, and the opportunities for making a complete fool of yourself are greater by far than in the shooting field as it all looks deceptively easy. Take a skeet layout for instance: there are two innocuous little boxy towers, called skeet houses, with a semi-circular path running between them. The skeet clays are thrown mechanically out of the towers on a regulated trajectory, at a regulated speed, singly or in pairs. You take a box of twenty-five cartridges and walk round the path, stopping off at each of the seven or eight predetermined positions; at each of these you are presented with two single clays and a pair thrown together. There are no surprises as everything is preordained. It's a doddle. Grown men have been reduced to tears trying to achieve a full score.

This reaction comes as no surprise given that most men are miles more competitive than most women. Men go out to shoot skeet (or 'Down the Line' – another very regulated, some might even say mind-numbing, discipline) – wearing jolly sexy little waistcoats made out of black neoprene with go-faster stripes and pockets and badges everywhere and the most amazingly lurid peaked caps bedecked with stickers saying things like 'I DONE BRILLIANT'. They crouch in rather anxious positions, like a dog caught

fouling the footpath, and then foam at the mouth when they miss small round clay objects thrown from a trap. Women don't shoot skeet, or Down the Line, much.

In the shooting field, too, men are much more assertive than women. On your average cocks-only day, even before they actually pick up a gun, there's a lot of what animal biologists call Male Aggression Behaviour going on at the meeting-place beforehand. It is one minute to nine. The car roars into the yard, scattering mud and chickens and narrowly missing the beaters' tractor which is on its way out. The man gets out, and lets the dog out of the back. (It's a strange thing but I don't recall ever seeing a man – however decent or well-bred he might be normally – actually OPEN THE CAR DOOR for a female companion when they arrive at a shoot. For dogs, yes; women, no. Odd, really.) He goes forward to greet his host and the other guns, at which point there is a lot of fairly wary chat on the lines of 'I SAY damned clever of you to have come on the back roads I had to do a hundred and thirty down the motorway thanks to all those wretched cones' and that sort of thing. Sizing each other up, really, like dogs. Establishing dominance. This takes about five minutes, during which time you sit mouse-like in the front seat and nobody notices. Then you hear the words *'Brought the old bag with me, hope you don't mind.'* This is the signal for you

to creep out of the far side of the car (he's neatly parked it so you step straight into a largeish puddle) and make your way round, under the unblinking gaze of the assembled males all standing about like cormorants on a rock. You wait to be introduced. As they say 'How do you do?' each man quickly looks you up and down (looking for WHAT? not VPL, surely) at which point your host immediately says 'Well'. Yes,' which is a real killer and means that the time allotted for social niceties is over and he wants to get on.

Sir Galahad then turns to you and in a venomous undertone hisses, 'WHY did you put that hat on I speCIFICALLY told you . . . what? well I can't help that it doesn't matter WHAT Mrs Thingy did what MATTERS is that you've made me look an utter fool God Almighty bloody DUCK BOTTOMS whatever must the old Colonel think now GET your act together and GET your boots on and be quick about it we're late and it's all YOUR FAULT.' Thus begins another lovely shooting day.

Apart from smashing his head in there and then or re-arranging his nether regions with your boot – tempting ideas both, and not totally without merit – you have three options. One is to explain later to your host, quietly and in private, that of course there are the most upsetting side-effects for a man on beta-blockers, according to Various Concerned Medical Opinions, and you're sure he understands just what you're referring to without your having to spell it out. This is quite a subtle move. The second option is just to stay at home and let him get on with it and pray (a) that the dog does something awful and (b) that a Strong Gale Force 9 is Imminent as he's forgotten to take his waterproofs. This may or may not work.

The third, and much the best, option is to take up shooting yourself. You will then be (grudgingly) allowed to wear the hat with the duck bottoms on it but only if you shoot not quite as well as (and of course under no circumstances whatsoever better than) he. I shoot worse than anyone I've ever met and can therefore be safely carted along or invited out by really good friends who are supportive and encouraging and never make me feel a twerp. After all, the whole point of any decent shooting party, ecology apart, is the bonhomie, not the bag.

Postscript. There is, come to think of it, a fourth alternative. Having taking up shooting yourself, get really good at it and then, eschewing the niceties of the shooting field, take up competitive clay shooting. It is, indisputably, Politically Correct. It can be done more or less comfortably at any time of the year. It is in a manner of speaking the sporting shot's equivalent of target shooting for the sporting-rifle shot, and (if you like that sort of thing) just as addictive.

Unlike Down the Line or skeet, Clay Pigeon Shooting Association-registered shoots will have all the variety of sporting clays but with a lot of extra tough bits thrown in, and they take place week in, week out, at registered meetings throughout the country. In order to qualify for them you have to shoot in a certain number of CPSA meetings; your combined score is computed and reviewed each September, you are then given a handicap and allotted to one of four classes according to your average score during the past year. You use an over-and-under gun (easier to sight than the shooting gentleman's side-by-side) and this can be choked at whim according to the course you are about to shoot. (You find yourself wishing that this applied to some of the participants in almost any shooting milieu.) You have smart box-bags of plastic-wadded cartridges, which shoot further and faster and more accurately than the felt-wadded ones you would carry in your grandfather's old cartridge bag on to the shooting field. And you wear padded waistcoats in neoprene and leather, rather than old Barbours and tweed coats. On a really tough competitive course of, say, 100 clays over 10 different stands, one of the handful of the country's top

CPSA shots *might* put up a score of between 85 and 95 out of 100 possible hits. Shooting with a side-by-side sporting shotgun, using felt-wadded cartridges as you would if out on a shoot, you would really be extremely pleased if you managed to make half marks, and it would be most unusual.

The difference between these CPSA shoots and your average social charity clay pigeon shoot is rather like the difference between a Jockey Club-registered race meeting, and a local hunt's point-to-point. The first is for the professional, the second for enthusiastic amateurs. Each is just as much fun, neither can be said to be better, or more 'correct' as a sport, but the first is inestimably tougher.

There are separate classes for women in CPSA shoots, but I can't say I've ever seen any of them wearing feathers, let alone duck bottoms, in their hats. The Mayerling look hasn't caught on there yet; but then equally, you wouldn't be seen dead wearing neoprene for a partridge shoot. Horses for courses . . . even in fashion.

A Bracing Day

Grouse shooting breeds horror stories. From the number of accidents that occur on grouse moors it seems surprising that the magic of the sport still endures, and yet for the really ardent shotgun enthusiast there is simply nothing more exciting, or rewarding, than a day in the butts with the birds coming over like the proverbial dingbats.

On the other hand, if you're not used to it, a day after grouse – driven or walked-up – can be something of a nightmare. We had a really nice young American professor to stay one year, who wasn't a shot but was wildly keen and bushy-tailed about his initiation into what he termed All This Scattish Sturf. He threw heaps of knitting into the river and thrashed the midges into a frenzy, followed stalking parties up the hill untidily but with gusto, pulled a gallant oar when asked, ate haggis without a murmur, was first up in the mornings and – the perfect guest – made early-morning tea for other people going out after roe at dawn. When left to his own devices he would be found buried in old copies of *The Field* as, he said, he wanted to get The Terminology Licked. It was all, he said, Just Great. Different, but Great. Very amiable, the American.

By that time it was the third week of August and we decided to have a go at walking the hills to see if there were any grouse around. Never enough to drive, there were usually enough for at least a day or two's walking-up which left everyone pleased with their efforts and completely knackered. No smart shoot, this, but a nice way of getting some exercise, perhaps eight or ten brace, and then having a picnic lunch and a swim in one of the little trout lochs up the hill before a quiet walk back.

In spite of the glories of the Twelfth, September is probably best for both driven and walked-up birds as by then the cheepers have grown and are just wild enough, and yet haven't been thinned out, nor have they congregated into packs as they do in October and November. In August they tend to sit tight, and guns and dogs can walk straight over them. All this had been explained to the nice American who took it in, nodded furiously, and said Gee and Golly and Let's Go Get 'Em.

And so we set off – seven guns, lots of enthusiastic children and eager young spaniels and various old and sage labradors with their old and sage handlers. So that he would have a better view of the proceedings (if there happened to be any) the American had been placed to walk in line between one of the guns and a keeper with a dog – in the middle of the line – and had been given detailed instructions about danger, safety, and the vital importance of keeping the line straight, walking neither too fast nor too slow, keeping an eye on his neighbours, stopping when a shot was fired, etc. etc. The keeper had given the usual pep talk to everyone before the party moved off, and the nice American muttered things like Wow and You Bet Your Ass. He was clearly going to be the very model of a modern major-general down to the tweed breeches which he'd been loaned and which he hadn't at first realised were meant to be done up tight below the knee, so he wore them 'long' and looked like an Egyptian gardener until he was set to rights over breakfast.

The first fifteen minutes of everyone's first day walking-up are always the most uncoordinated. You have forgotten since last year how to put one foot in front of another, what it is like to churn through heather, bracken, peat bogs, scree, gullies, burns and banks; the dogs are fresh out of the kennels and raring to go and the sweet heather-scented air is full of 'Come-here-ya-bugger' admonishments; children are overexcited and understretched. You have to watch where you're going, where everyone else is going, what the dogs are doing, where your feet are, where everyone else is – it's purgatory.

After about twenty minutes, though, you get into the rhythm of the thing. The line has settled down; you no longer find one small soul lagging behind to pick blaeberries, or someone else, wind in the hair at the top of the hill, striding out and having to be yelled at from below; the affair has developed nicely into something resembling an ordered advance, there's less chat as people begin to feel the miasmal effect of kippers or too much kedgeree for breakfast after the previous night's heavy conversation with the Taylor's or the malt, and the keepers are feeling less vulnerable. And this was a perfect day for it: warm but with a breeze, a herd of red deer away on the high tops, pipits and warblers flicking over the bloomy heather, ravens tumbling under the bluebell sky, sheep grazing and trotting away in front of us – a perfect day.

The American had had something of a shaky start. He'd lost a borrowed wellington boot to start with in the first burn (by the vehicles); he then flung himself bodily over every tussock and bump as if they were moguls on the piste; then put on a great spurt and got screamed at or forgot what he was meant to be doing and stopped to take photographs and got screamed at again. But it didn't seem to faze him in the least. 'Say, this is Just Fantastic, my my, but this is Just Something,' he would mutter every so often, ploughing on with great gusto, a real goer, totally undeterred. The line would stop every so often to wait for him or to bring him back into the fold, and he was gradually getting the hang of it. We still hadn't seen a single bird – they were sitting very tight – the day was getting hotter (we had started out late and it was almost midday), and there was quite a lot of discussion up and down the line as to who had put on too much clothing and which bit they were going to take off at the next halt.

Then one of the dogs scented something. 'Steady now sir' muttered the keeper on the American's left, as the gun on his right came to a stop and all watched the spaniel beavering back and forth with huge enthusiasm ahead of them. 'Dog's found something in front, be ready now sir, close in on the right, go on just a step or two there . . .' and the line inched forward, guns at the ready.

Later on, the American explained that he thought that the phrase 'Dog's found something' meant – as it might well have done if you were in, say, Brooklyn – that the dog had found some old bones, or some nice dead thing in which to roll, which presumably implied that we would all have to stop again and wait until it had sorted itself out. He reckoned that this would therefore be the ideal moment in which to remove some small stones which, thanks to an earlier contretemps with a bit of scree, had lodged themselves inside his boot. The rest of the line had come warily to a halt: there was a small mound of heather directly in front of him and he thought he could therefore make the most of a God-given chance to stop and deal with his particular problem while the rest of the party took a break and watched the dog doing whatever dogs do. He therefore stepped smartly forward to the mound, turned his back to it and sat down. Seventeen birds got up as one, going like Scud missiles in all directions; the two

neighbouring guns let fly, keepers shouted 'Behind', children yelled 'In front', the rest of the line cheered encouragement and there was a yell, like a banshee's, of terror, and all that could be seen of the nice American professor was a pair of wellington boots stuck upside down in the heather.

There was a terrible silence; then everyone was running or unloading guns, sprinting up or down the hill to where he'd fallen. The old keeper came thundering past me gasping out 'Och fer God's sake the poor mannie,' and I had lightning visions of headlines in the *Glasgow Herald*. A child's voice, clear as a bell, came up from below, fretful and afraid, asking what had happened . . . Then out of the heather emerged a face, white and aghast.

He clambered to his feet spitting out bits of local flora and covered in grouse droppings, unscathed but shaking. 'Wh . . . wh . . . what HAPPENED, did I do something wrong or what?' he gibbered. The sight of him safe and sound, the relief, was too much: the whole line, to a man, shouted and whooped, threw their hats in the air and whistled – the keepers, the beaters, the guns, the whole party erupted, and the American stared as the first dawn of realisation crept over his face.

'Jeeesus H. KeRIST what the FUCK's going ON?' he screamed, banging his hands against his sides in impotent rage and causing a cloud of midges to rise up in surprise. 'For GOD'S sake you guys, when you said out front you never said it was going to be THAT sort of out front. I mean for crying out loud all I do is sit down and everyone starts SHOOTing and what the HELL are you laughing at I thought I was DEAD . . .'

When he left the following week, he took a brace of birds away with him as he felt it was appropriate that they should be properly stuffed. His command of English terminology had improved sufficiently, he said, for him really to appreciate that.

Cocks Only

An editor of a monthly magazine once rang me up and, without further ado (no nice preambles, no chit-chat, but then of course their time is mega-bucks, whereas I like to ease myself slowly into a situation, as into a hot bath) said: 'We want you to write something funny about shooting by the end of the month,' and put the phone down.

I thought about it for a bit, rang him back, told him there was nothing remotely funny about shooting even by the end of the month, and put the phone down.

It is in fact true: there are of course funny situations, or funny characters, or funny incidents connected with shooting, just as there must be hysterically funny moments connected with just about anything – golf, pot-holing or even knitting, for all I know – but of itself the thing is deadly serious. Once you have stood in a grouse butt and listened to your aged host, purple in the face and hyperventilating over some poor young guest who has had the misfortune not to have connected properly with the feathered missiles whistling over the heather at him in an October gale, *and been noticed*, you know it's not funny. 'Will SOMEbody tell that BLOODY idiot I didn't ask him all the way up here to join my friends and drink my port and then wave his bloody gun around in the air like some damned pooftah paintah fella and MISS – dammit man, didn't they teach you ANYthing?' And then, in a loud aside to one of his ancient cronies in the next butt: 'Trouble with all these bloody schoolboys, no proper education, that's what – had one fella up last year for the cull, friend of the children's don't you know, top score in the Ashburton Shield, couldn't hit a barn door at sixty yards. Keeper frightfully upset, fella came back to the house and po'try all next day, I ask you. Lefties, all of em.'

And woe betide anyone firing what might be remotely perceived as a marginally unsafe shot. Quite right too, really; but I do remember one lovely crisp day in the first week of December, when we were waiting for pheasants in a large wood. The weather was perfect and the woodcock were in: every drive produced a dozen or more flitting and jinxing through the rhododendrons, which was wonderful except for the fact that amongst the party there was an Italian who hadn't shot very much before, and certainly had no idea of how to shoot at all. The woodcock came dancing through the branches, there were strangled cries from the beaters of 'W'COCK forWARD', everyone was shooting, or yelling 'Yours' to everyone else, and the Italian got thoroughly overexcited, blasting off in all directions and felling the odd sapling. This meant that whoever had been placed next to him spent most of the drive face down on the ground and praying. Finally it became too much: one very senior member of the party, who hadn't moved fast enough and had turned to find himself looking down a

pair of barrels, let out an enraged roar, marched over to the Italian and got him by the throat. 'You do that just one more time you filthy foreign swine,' he yelled, 'and I'll shoot back. And I'm a better bloody shot than you.'

At the next drive the Italian, thoroughly chastened, was despatched to stand by himself out of harm's way in a field outside the next bit of wood. In spite of the fact that he had certainly been a menace, and could have been lethal, and *some*one had to tell him, I felt rather sorry for him. He had actually had a rotten day, mostly due to the fact that he didn't really understand what he was meant to be doing or how to do it; certainly he didn't have an inkling about what he should or should not be firing at. When you take into consideration the fact that they shoot almost anything in certain parts of Italy, it wasn't surprising; but it did mean that the rest of us, when not flattened on the ground, spent most of the time screaming instructions at him from the next peg or two away. 'No Antonio, you don't shoot thrushes in this country . . . No Antonio, it's a seagull . . . ANTONIO NO . . . Cats no, Antonio, blackbirds no, and NO ROEDEER WITH A GUN, OK? Pheasants, right? Forget about the woodcock, forget about EVERYthing else, just concentrate on the pheasants – there, large dark bird, long tail, like that, right? . . . Good, and only in FRONT . . . Oh, and up AGAINST THE SKY, OK?'

He seemed to have got the hang of it finally, and was obviously relieved – as indeed was everyone else – that he had been put to stand by himself out of sight in the field, from whence came not a sound. The drive proceeded, everyone relaxed and enjoyed themselves. finally, in the midst of much firing in the line (they were good birds that day, the wind was just right), a couple of fast shots were heard from the direction of the field (he'd obviously been surprised by something, and had let both barrels off almost as one). At the end of the drive the keeper therefore climbed over the fence at the edge of the wood, calling out

– more as a matter of routine than with any great hope – 'Anything to pick up sir?' and was met by silence. Fearing the worst, we all ran over to the fence and peered out into the field.

There, partly hidden in the tall rushes by the edge, was Antonio on his hands and knees, burying something.

Casting a terrified glance at the keeper, and at the man who had nearly strangled him an hour or so before, and at the rest of the party who were all gazing at him in open-mouthed astonishment, Antonio, ashen-white and in a welter of confusion, began to babble like a stream. He was 'Very sorry, eh? butta theesa birda came out whizzaa likea thata, an' I no see wella what eet ees, and I shoota an' 'ee fall, an ees nota pheasan', sorry, eh? beega mistake . . . an' I theenk eef I hide 'eem in de earth ees abetta, no?'

During a grouse shooting party at Glenfeshie, on September the 9th of 1836, a Mr Golding 'shot what he claimed was an eagle and which turned out to be, once retrieved from the hole into which it had fallen, a horned sheep.' The gamekeeper didn't think much of the proceedings and was reputed to have said that 'he had been 15 years in the habit of attending gentlemen shooting, but had never seen the like before.'

That night we opened the champagne. Antonio, to his own and everyone else's utter amazement, had finally fired a legitimate shot, and had brought down the one and only blackcock of the week.

The Auld Bugger

It is the sheer *variety* of shooting that is one of the things that makes it such a delight. You can go after dove in Mexico or guineafowl in Africa, duck in Patagonia or quail in Georgia, francolin in Spain or Mongolian pheasants in Mongolia, I imagine, but you don't actually really have to go so far afield to enjoy your shooting days – there is enough variety in these islands to keep you busy for a lifetime. There are smart shoots in rolling landscapes, and non-smart shoots where you spend most of the day hacking through the undergrowth; there are snipe in Irish bogs, and grouse on Scottish moors, and pheasants like steeplejacks in Devon hills. There are woodcock wisping through shadows, partridges that explode over high fences on wide bright days with the stubble glinting; there are fields of kale with low sun in your eyes, or waiting for pigeon in high winds, or teal whistling down the horizontal rain at dusk.

And, always, a wealth of things to watch and see – dogs working a hill, trees burnished in an October sun, a quick Brittany spaniel watching pigeon from a hide, an old dog fox sneaking away down a hedge, rabbits bolting out on long fields. And then, of course, the first bird, on the first drive of the day, and everyone is watching . . .

And then there is stalking – each time different, memorable, astonishing. We went out at first light one lovely September dawn to look for roebuck – usually a four-hour stint, back in time for a quick bath and a good breakfast before going out again. Twelve hours later, at four in the afternoon, we lurched into the gun room having got not a roe but four stags out of the forestry, and a wild goat by the shore. Or the first stalk ever, with the sun straight behind the beast; or going out for the hind cull in the snow on Boxing Day having stayed up all night, praying for bed, Panadol and oblivion; stalking the woodlands or the gut-wrenching hills, turning back for home at the end of the day, a job well done and the long walk back a delight to be savoured with a fine companion . . .

There are times, of course, when it all goes horribly wrong – it's never always the picture-book scenario – but then, the bad days, the dramas, the unorthodox stalks, perhaps these remain as amongst the most memorable.

Early one autumn, a call came through from one of the local farmers saying that there were some marauding stags which had clearly got through the deer fence and were beating the daylights out of his crops, and would someone come down and sort out the problem? (It is important to do this fast, otherwise the farmer gets understandably shirty and then there are even bigger problems and it all ends in tears.)

For the following five days the first moments of daylight would find Donald and I, having got comfortably into position in a ditch or cowering behind a knoll or bunched up against a wall, hoping to catch the beasts, who would have come out of a plantation (where they'd taken up residence in 5-star comfort, away from the harsh life of the hills) into the big field behind the farmhouse. There were five of them. Marauding stags get twitchy – perhaps they have a conscience after all and know they're where they ought not to be – so it wouldn't be a question of having to get the whole lot, one stag shot and the rest would get the message and clear off somewhere else to find food. The farmer was quite right, the five stags were definitely there – they were always there, browsing and munching at every hour of the day but, curiously, only when you drove past without a rifle, or when it was Sunday.

That week was the longest week of my life: out every dawn, waiting for the errant stags. Perhaps we had spooked them, or perhaps they were just mind-readers, but every single time, just as daylight broke barely enough to be able to see through the telescope sight, there would be a burst of activity, a heap of antlers would jump the fence back into the plantation, and that was that. Perhaps they were ghosts.

But this was getting stupid, and Donald was not the man to be outwitted by a bunch of stags, for heaven's sake. They couldn't be that clever, after all. Tomorrow we'd get them. We'd build a hide out of straw bales, go out after midnight, and just wait up all night for the damned things. They had to come out into the field, he reckoned, about 2.30 or 3.00 and we'd be waiting for them this time, not trying to creep up on them when they were already out. No messing about. The farmer was getting marginally unpleasant about the whole affair and clearly Donald felt that his reputation as the finest stalker in Scotland was at stake. This was going to be done properly.

We spent five minutes the previous evening building a hide two bales long, one bale wide and a couple of bales across the top in case of rain – nothing fancy, and gaps everywhere for what the mercenaries might call Good All-Round Visibility. The farmhouse was right by the glen road, and the field was right behind the farmhouse, so we wouldn't lose the hide when we came back in the dark. Duly, midnight gone, Donald and I set off again to drive the half-hour down the glen road, armed with a torch, ther-moses of tea and coffee, Mars Bars and some sandwiches. Well-equipped, efficient (we forgot the rifle and had to go back for it), Hereford would have been proud of us. We turned off the road and backed into the farmyard (always, according to the manual, have the car parked in a getaway position), got out all the gear, and walked up to the gate leading out into the field to spy carefully, to check that the wind had not altered and, as far as a cloudy half-moon would permit, to ensure that the beasts had not yet come out into the field. We then crept out to the hide some 60 yards away, dragged the roof on and settled in for the night watch.

It was too dark to see the fence, of course, but you could just make out the edge of the plantation some 200 yards away. The wind was just right, coming towards us from the plantation and, as long as that didn't change, it was going to be a cinch.

We talked in whispers for the next three hours, keeping watch the meanwhile. One person would spy through the gaps, the other would pour tea (we'd already unwrapped the Mars Bars beforehand, so they wouldn't crackle), test the wind again, light a cigarette, make sure the hide wasn't on fire. Half an hour, and we'd swap duties. We talked and talked – it's quite hard to remember to whisper, especially if you're laughing, but we did jolly well. Nothing came to interrupt us. Three-thirty is a bad time as you start to flag then, so we had the Mars Bars and opened the coffee flask. The inside of the hide seemed to be all thistle, I was aching to have a pee, it was cold and the moon kept on getting smothered in clouds, but still nothing had come into the field. Surely, in the next hour or so, something would appear.

Four o'clock, the first silver light broke in the east. Hares came out to wash their faces; the clouds changed colour quietly, slowly; a roe deer came through the fence, a doe, and began to pick her way delicately through the grasses, to be followed by her kid. They grazed for about twenty minutes, then disappeared again. The midges came out. Birds started on their wake-up-call routine, the dawn was getting on with its business of looking lovely, another hour or so had passed and still no stags.

I was getting lightheaded. Was that an antler in the plantation? What was that movement by the fence? An old cock pheasant, wary but busy by himself. Birds sat on the top wire getting warm in the pale light, the wind was still coming from where it had been all night, and Donald's stomach was making thunderous noises. It was like being in the middle of a herd of elephants. Time for the sandwiches, which someone had sat on. It couldn't be long now, for heaven's sake, before they would appear, silently, and surprise us. We knew them well, having seen them so often in the field in broad daylight; the big one with the long wild swept-back tops and the shortish bey points, a nice old 14-pointer, must be fifteen or so, carrying his head low; his companion, not as good a head but a big heavy beast, very dark, with shorter thicker points and a longer face, younger by probably four to five years; and then the three younger ones who always seemed to keep together – one nice small royal, what Donald called a 'nice ladies' head', and the two others – all of whom must have been about six or seven years old – decent rectangular heads that would develop into something good in a few years, breeding heads for the future. 'If you see the old one, take him, he's got a limp and he's going back.'

It was claustrophobic in the hide, we had to keep shuffling about as bits went numb or cramp set in. Through the gaps in the bales we watched the farmhouse coming to life behind us, the lights going on upstairs, the kitchen door flung open and the hens running up to it. Away in the distance dogs started to bark and the farmers' programme blared out of an open window. Another hour passed.

Seven o'clock, the postman's van. Stops for a chat by the kitchen door in the yard, laughter, drives off. Sound of tractors moving off up the glen road. Someone driving a Land-Rover, you could hear it crashing over the cattle-grid a mile or so away. More coffee. 'Let's give it another hour? Just in case?'

By nine o'clock we'd had it. The sun was bright and cheerful, the road bustling with activity; the garbage lorry had been and gone, clattering the old metal rubbish bins by the roadside; I knew I couldn't have even held the rifle up, let alone steady, if anything appeared (which it certainly wasn't going to do now). I had rigor mortis in places I didn't even know existed, Donald had run out of cigarettes and was evincing severe withdrawal symptoms, I'd got through all mine hours ago, the bottom of the hide looked like a parrot cage, I knew every bit of straw in those bales in a totally intimate fashion, the whole thing had been fruitless and, apart from the fun of actually doing it, a wash-out. We staggered out of the hide, throwing bales to right and left. We stretched, and groaned with pain as limbs and muscles were suddenly galvanised after the hours of cramp. Suddenly aware that normal talk was possible after so long whispering, we whooped and shouted like idiots let out of shackles.

We walked back drunkenly (the pins and needles were torture) the 60 yards to the farmhouse. Donald relieved himself by the wall, I found a friendly bramble bush. We both fumbled about with rifle-slips and thermoses, and made our way over to the car moaning and complaining to each other. Donald shouted out through the kitchen door, lots of cheerful banter, a wave of sheepdogs flowing out of the barn smiling and making friendly 'good-morning-and-how-lovely-to-SEE-you' yowly noises, hens complaining and getting flurried out of the way, the car door screeching on a duff hinge. I dropped the box of bullets and everything spilled everywhere and Donald, having unloaded the rifle and put it into the back seat and turning round to climb wearily into the driver's seat while berating me for my stupidity, fell suddenly, clumsily, to the ground.

God almighty, I thought, panicking, he's had a seizure, I don't have the arnica, now what? help, and stumbled round the back of the car to pick him up. He was lying on his front with his arm pointing forward and in a large patch of dung. In the voice of one just recently arrived from the dead, he was whispering hoarsely. Perhaps it was a stroke. I flumped down beside him to hear. 'Look, bloody hell, LOOK,' he croaked.

I looked. The car had been backed into the farmyard, some 20 yards from the entrance to the road. On the other side of the road, beyond the statutory wire fence, was a small stretch of scrubby grass with some sheep on it, and a duckpond in the middle surrounded by whin bushes. Beyond the duckpond was a 3- or 4-acre patch of turnips and, behind that, some Forestry Commission woods. There, 120 yards away, surrounded by noise and clatter and tractor sounds and voices and people moving around and dogs and general bustle and the smell of bacon wafting out of the farmhouse kitchen, the big old stag stood in the field of turnips intent on his own breakfast. Unperturbed, and downwind.

When we talked it over after, it was obvious that he'd skirted round the plantation we'd been watching so carefully, had come out on to the road half a mile further down, jumped the fence on the other side and come up quietly into the turnip field. Given the fact that he'd obviously been there some time, and was evidently not too bothered by human activity, all we really had to do was to walk boldly out into the road and take him from there. But after an eight-hour long vigil, followed by the frenzy of seeing him, and in the wrong place, we weren't either of us thinking all that clearly. What we did instead (after I had scrabbled round on the ground picking up spilled cartridges, had carefully opened the car door from the supine position to get the rifle out, and loaded it with shaking hands while Donald lay there moaning and whispering things like Och Bloody Hell and Fer God's Sake Move Woman Move Yer Hurdies and other helpful exhortations) what we did do, probably out of force of habit, was a complicated and totally non-textbook approach which involved a toes-and-elbows creep across to the entrance of the farmyard (forgetting the wind which was mercifully also carrying the bacon smells across from behind us out to the field opposite), through the slurry and the astonished chickens; a slow painstaking crawl out across the road – to the amazement of the sheep inside the fence, all of whom, it appeared, were too fascinated to move – on to knees now agonisingly punctured by loose gravel chippings from the potholed tarmac, so as to use one of the bins as a rest to steady (as far as was possible) a shot through the wire strands of the fence.

It was, undoubtedly, the most undignified stalk of Donald's career. But it worked, and the beast went down like a stone. Donald clapped me on the shoulder and sat down heavily in the road. I was shaking like a leaf. His face broke into a huge grin, he took off his cap and shook his head. 'Well I'll be damned, wifey,' he said. 'To think we've been out all night, we've spent over eight hours in yon effing hide, and then to get him in broad daylight, with the wind behind us, off a bloody dustbin. Fer cryin out loud, the auld bugger eh?'

The game book that night had a lot written into it, with age, and points, and weight, and what-have-you. The location was noted as Dustbin 2, Glen Road. But this time, the stag had a name.

Driven to Distraction

T o be in a car driven by my father used to be my idea of hell. A mild-mannered, even placid, man of unutterable charm and good humour and with a delicious sense of the ridiculous on terra firma, he turned into a raving lunatic behind the wheel. And he simply hated it when other people drove, although for some inexplicable reason he was very good with complete novices, and gave me my first driving lessons down Irish country lanes in which we invariably ended up in the ditch but only because we were both laughing so much. My mother, however, had not driven him since 1954, when apparently he swore at her, demanded to change places and take the wheel himself and got out to perform this manoeuvre, whereupon she drove off leaving him stranded, after a very good party in Dublin, at 5.00 in the morning, in a white tie and a thunderstorm, 20 miles from home. He hitched a lift from a passing milk float and was dropped at the gates, walked up the drive, had a bath and never mentioned the incident afterwards.

My father drove like Toad, with an unshakeable and oft-repeated conviction both in his own supreme ability and in the utter crassness of every other motorist. 'Damned idiot' he would mutter, braking sharply; there would be a huge crunching sound behind, as five cars piled into one another and everyone sat on their horns. 'See that? Pretty piece of driving there, man should be convicted . . . Hi, LOOK OUT, bloody fool' he would shout, mounting the pavement to avoid a bus and frightening an old lady, who would drop her shopping bag and dive for cover into a shop window, smashing the glass. 'Ah well, what can you expect, man's a cretin, not an inkling . . . . hey YOU, we USE INDICATORS

IN THIS COUNTRY YOU KNOW' he'd bellow at some astonished motorcyclist, purple in the face and gesticulating furiously out of the window and only narrowly avoiding having his arm removed by a passing bollard. 'Whhhhhh . . . .' (sharp intake of breath, always a bad sign) 'ah well, it was only JUST red, and that ass of a woman had no business at all coming through the other lights like that, could have hit me straight on if I hadn't moved so fast; got to have reflexes like lightning,' he'd confide, swerving wildly to avoid a pedestrian and causing an oncoming lorry to swerve in turn and hit a parked car. 'God almighty, did you SEE that half-wit? I tell you, it's just not safe driving these days.'

He loved his own car, a dented and very ancient Rover, with a passion, and went out every evening to see that it was all right and tuck it up for the night. He always referred to a car as 'she'. 'Going well isn't she?' he'd sing out happily as we hurtled down motorways (once actually in the wrong direction). 'Oh yes, lovely, hooray for the open road'. He had read all of Dornford Yates and clearly imagined himself in the title role of the Berry books (having owned, at one time or another, a series of big old drophead coupés) and would lean over as he took corners, double-declutching *con brio*: all that 'the great car leapt forward' stuff made him go misty eyed, like the National Anthem.

He smoked while driving. Bicyclists leapt off their machines and fell into ditches, just like in films, as we swept past, veering wildly while he busied himself removing his gloves, lighting up, opening the window. He also had a rather unnerving habit of taking both hands off the wheel in order to ferret about in his back pockets looking for the old red flat packet of Dunhills, usually when accelerating uphill and overtaking something on the brow. Woe betide you if you flinched, or stamped your foot on imaginary brakes, or screamed. Or, as I did once, grabbed the steering wheel. 'Now look here' he thundered, as we wrestled furiously. 'I've been driving since long before you were born and nobody, BUT NOBODY, has ever done that in my car and I WON'T HAVE IT, do you understand? I was perfectly in control and . . . . oh dear. Damn. Ah well . . . Um . . .' (reversing carefully out of a large oak back into the main road and the path of an oncoming school bus filled with the faces of screaming children). 'NOW look what you've made me do, don't you REALISE how dangerous that might have been? Now where are those wretched cigarettes I was looking for before you started all this kerfuffle? – ah here we are, that's better.' And we'd lurch off again, he humming a little hum like Pooh to show he'd regained his composure, and me duly chastened and praying for home.

I've been frightened by lots of people's driving but with time you become immune to the terrors and learn to sit in the back seat and go to sleep whenever possible, and to keep quiet. Although it's quite a good way of losing weight, actually: letting someone else drive the car on your own home ground is brilliant, the inches just pour off. I discovered this interesting medical fact after going out stalking with some German tenants one day.

We'd had a lovely day. We had walked for miles, the hills were looking wonderful, deer were milling about everywhere as it was just the beginning of the rut, the stalker was pleased, the Germans were ecstatic. Each had finally, after a good and exciting stalk, been presented with a shootable stag, one of which had been a fine old 13-pointer. The two had originally drawn lots as to who should take the first stalk and the first shot, and the older man, who'd drawn second, had got the 13-pointer. He was so pleased with himself that he could hardly get the words out, kept on chuntering away to his chum on the long walk back to the vehicles and burbling fairly incoherently to me and to the stalker at the same time. 'Iss so good, *nicht wahr*? a vunderful valking ve haf, unt zen a vunderful how you say *ja* stalk sank you, und ze rifle she is goot but Cheeses Greist I do werry fantastich *ja*?' And so he went on. Nothing better than a satisfied tenant.

Once back by the minibus, we opened the flask and gave them a dram, explaining that this was the Highland way of celebrating a stag. Not on the hill, mind, but afterwards once you'd got back to the car. This was also, clearly, a Good Thing and they drained the flask between them. The pony boy and the horse had walked back with us, we all heaved the beasts into the trailer behind the stalker's van, packed everything away and then I opened the driver's door of the minibus to climb in. 'No, no, NO, iss a Volkswagen wan, *nein*? A Charman wehicle. I, ze Charman, will conduct no problem. Get in back pliss.' I did. It's much easier not to argue especially with a rather senior 6-foot man who's already made up his mind. And no man really wants to be driven by a woman.

There was quite a lot of to-ing and fro-ing as he turned the thing round – we'd parked in a farmyard and there were great heaps of dung and crud everywhere. Another of his compatriots had cleverly overturned the van off the ramp and into a huge pit of silage only the previous week, and there were still the marks of footprints on the inside of the roof where they'd all had to exit upside-down out of the side windows . . . Then the road home was easy, and empty, and the light was still good. Old Schumacher at the wheel was obviously having fun proving his mastery of the machine, with complete disregard for verges, and a lot of crunching the gears round corners without using the clutch which is apparently the way they drive in rallies, and taking the cattle-grids all along the glen road at great speed so that they roared. I was well past caring, and looking forward to a hot bath, and sat back with one eye open just for show in case he checked in the rear mirror, thinking my own thoughts as he went wittering on to his friend beside him in the front.

Not far to go now, up the brae, then a sharpish corner and down past another farm, then we'd be on the straight main road and home in about ten minutes, He came roaring up to the wiggle in the road. 'Bit of a tight bend here,' I remarked conversationally – I didn't want it to

sound like I was worried or anything, even though we were going like the clappers – you usually took this about at about 20, and then only if you were really pushing it. '*Ja ja*' came back the laconic reply as he put his foot on the brake, at which point all four wheels hit a large patch of slurry and the van went into a monumental skid.

He completely lost it. We went careering sideways round the bend (luckily there wasn't a soul or another vehicle in sight) and down the steep slope on the other side, the farm buildings were looming up, I was crouching down with only my eyeballs above the waterline and clinging on to everything I'd got, he was finally getting it together, braking in spurts and trying to hang on to the steering wheel and, as I saw the buildings all coming closer, I screamed out 'WATCH THE CORNER . . .'

It was a totally stupid thing to say. The trouble with trying to get an idea across, fast, to someone who is not one hundred percent relaxed and conversant with the vernacular is that the meaning tends to get screwed up. There wasn't any time to explain anyway as, horridly pale and with a rictus of terror across his face, he held on as we juddered and slewed towards the side of the farm buildings. Added to which, the Germans are a very obedient race. They don't argue with orders at important moments. A Spaniard would have found time to turn round and hit me, an Italian would have been screaming so hard he wouldn't have heard me anyway. But I'd said something with a degree of authority, so the German did it. To the letter. We hit the corner full on, and once again I found myself wrapped round an outhouse.

Before we'd set off I had, by the grace of God, reminded them both to do up their seats belts. We all staggered out of the steaming, wrecked machine quite miraculously unscathed. Much later, I tried to explain what I'd meant but by then, of course, it was history. I weighed myself when we finally got home, and I'd lost 4 pounds that day.

Tooth and Claw

W hen he was about twenty-five, my father shot a tiger in India. The skin lay around the house for as long as I can remember, complete with the head which had its mouth open in a roar and, with its startling white fangs, inflicted untold damage to bare feet if you happened to meet it round the passages in the dark. My father always maintained that it was real stroke of luck that he had got the tiger rather than the other way round. He'd fired at it from up a tree – in which he was waiting under a full moon with a somewhat less enthusiastic goat for company tied below – and, thanks to a passing cloud which obliterated the moonlight at the precise moment he let off his shot, he had merely wounded the tiger instead of killing it outright. The tiger, justifiably incensed, had started to climb the tree to settle the score so my father, with the alacrity, he said, of youth, army training and sheer terror, leapt out of the tree and found himself in a small thorn bush below, in which he was swiftly joined by the tiger. They then performed what he described as an elaborate game of grandmother's footsteps round and round the bush. Then the moon came out, the tiger came round the bush in the opposite direction, and that was that.

He had had an extremely varied shooting career. He called and shot leopard (apparently they sound like someone sawing wood) and had hunted wild boar in the Iraqi marshes and gazelle in Tibet, whence he had ridden from India over the mountains. He had chanced upon some charming locals who were out hunting and who had insisted that he should join in. (They used rifles with what sounded like thin metal sledges attached to the underside of the stock which, being springy, allowed you to lie down and follow the leaps and bounds of the quarry across the landscape.) And crocodile, and buffalo, and all the things that young men were supposed to shoot in the 1930s.

His mother, six months great with child, had been taken off by my grandfather to shoot snow leopard in India, so I suppose it was in the blood. But although he was a good shot with a rifle, he really loved his scatterguns best. I have pictures of him and my mother on a goose shoot on the Hortobàgyi Plain, both wearing the swineherd's long full-skirted sheepskin coats and standing beside one of the hides by the shallow lakes – a large hole cut out of the stiff damp clay. And later, during the war, in 1940 in the Middle East, more photographs of him shooting sandgrouse, in uniform and spats ('during a lull in the fighting', he explained), and others of what look like wonderful parties

out in the desert where they went for francolin and quail and duck, the local bedouin acting as beaters.

Later on in Ireland there were (with the exception of the tiger-skin) no trophies in the house – everyone was far too busy going off to the Slobs for geese, or traipsing over the bogs for snipe, or shooting one another's pheasants, or hunting and fishing, to bother about hanging dead things on a wall. (Apart from the inevitable fox brush in the cloakroom.) However, I do remember the house of a very eccentric neighbour where there was a proper 'trophy room'. To a child, it was the most terrifying place, especially in winter when the electricity would blow and monsters would peer glassily off the walls into the gloom. There was a ghastly huge hippo over the door; elk, buffalo and wildebeeste scowled out of corners and a cheetah lay curled, apparently in earnest conversation with a python, round the base of a floor-lamp. There were skins of every conceivable size and hue – mottled, spotted, striped and variegated – all suffering from mange, over the furniture and the floor; there were poor beaked things in glass cases and a swordfish over the sofa; and a collection of tails hanging off the bottom of a lampshade which, made of finest vellum, I was assured was human skin. And a glass of false teeth in the bookshelves. 'Ah yes, sure dat fella put up de fiercest fight of dem all,' the owner used to confide in me, tapping conspiratorially at the glass. And of course, aged six, I believed him with a ghoulish fascination. I later discovered that, a highly intelligent and successful writer, he had never hunted anything except women all his life, and had collected all these things from old film studios.

A generation later in Scotland my daughter, then also aged six, wrote a long letter to Father Christmas asking for, amongst other things, some owl pellets. She'd written 'PLEASE' in capitals and heavily underlined so it was obviously an item of some significance. My husband, deeply ensconced in back numbers of *The Economist*, was no help so I enlisted the aid of the local poacher, Fergus, a man of considerable resources, to show me where the barn owls were living in an old forester's hut, and a shoe-box of deeply unattractive bits and pieces duly appeared on Christmas morning. My daughter was overjoyed. Fergus, whose complicity in the matter was of course never divulged, subsequently became one of her greatest friends and the two of them would take off on forays, returning with unspeakable things in plastic bags, and all over the house you'd come across little caches of skulls, feathers, strange stones, skins and odd bones. The worst of these I discovered when I opened up the deepfreeze one day and found, lying on top of the ice cream and the raspberries, a large cowpat labelled 'Interesting FOOD don't touch' and a seriously-ex chough.

To be fair about it her grasp of biology improved no end, according to rather stunned school reports, and the activities of the birds and the bees held no terrors for her. 'Gosh did you KNOW Mummy ... they do it BACKwards ... and Fergus says it doesn't hurt a BIT . . .' My husband, boss-eyed, never uttered, but later roundly accused me of not exerting enough discipline, and encouraging too much frivolity and *licence*, into his daughter's education. Many years later she was doing her university entrance, and they had gone off to a bookshop together. She said she was looking for a copy of *The Rape of the Lock*, and he exploded. 'That's it,' he shouted at her in fury, 'that's the absolute END. Your mother taught you about the facts of life when you were FAR too young and SEE where it's got you. I won't have such books in the house and that's THAT.' Luckily she knew that he had read PPE at Oxford rather than English, so just laughed merrily at this, whereupon it took apparently a good half-hour to explain and calm him down.

Fergus remained a guiding force in her introduction to the natural world. He certainly had an uncanny way with animals, could croon roosting pheasants into falling out of trees, would set wings and broken bones, sing to seals on the shore and conjure fish from the deep when required. Rumour was that he had been a vet, and then decided he'd rather live like a tramp in his beloved wilderness. He always looked as if he'd had birds nesting in him, with twigs and bits of dead egg and shell all down the front of his threadbare pullover, one arm of which was a strange peaty shade of brown as if he'd just removed it from the backside of a cow. He smelt atrocious. But he could recite McGonagall, and the Ballad of MacAlasdair, played the mouth-organ and was a brilliant carver – the walls of his bothy were hung with fiddles and clock-cases that he'd made, as well as bits of carcasses that were 'jus' bidin' their time like, afore gettin' cured'. He slept, he told me, with a deerskin as an underblanket to keep out the cold. He was always followed by three of the mangiest lurchers imaginable, and the pot on the stove was never empty. 'Come on in mum, there's a fine bit o' dinner burbolatin' there . . . ' but I never had the courage to sample anything after he confided once that the merrily bubbling pot contained what he described as 'a bit o' gull and some disinterrogated rabbit'. Perhaps the lurchers had had an off day.

In 1806 in Dalmatia, when the Napoleonic Wars had resulted in a dire lack of food, the really generous host would allow his guest to choose, for himself, which cat he would like for his dinner. Some seventy years later Captain Burnaby, on his great ride to Khiva, tells how his faithful follower whispered in his ear: 'We are to have a great feast tonight. The guide's brother-in-law has a horse which is not very well, and we are to eat him.' 'Will there be anything else?' Burnaby enquired hopefully. 'Why no,' came the reply of the astonished Tartar, 'what more would you have? We might eat two sheep at a time, but a horse . . . no.'

The Ballad of MacAlasdair

Clansmen, the peats are burning bright;
Sit round then in a ring
And I will tell you of the night
I danced before the King.
For as a dancer in my youth
So great was my renown
The King himself invited me
To dance in London town.

My brand-new presentation kilt
And ornaments I wore,
And with my *sgian dubh* I rapped
Upon the Palace door.
And presently some Earl, or Duke,
Came down the Palace stair,
And to the keyhole put his eye
Demanding who was there.

'Open the door' I sternly cried
'As quickly as you can.
Is this the way that you receive
A Highland gentleman?'
The door was opened wide and word
Went round: 'MacAlasdair is here' –
And all the Palace did resound
With one tremendous cheer.

And all the ladies of the Court
In pearls and jewels bedecked
Did blush and tremble when my name
Was spoke with great respect.
Slowly at first, with hands on hips,
I danced with ease and grace,
Then raised my hands above my head
As faster grew my pace.

At last no human eye could see
My feet sae fast and quick,
And from the floor great clouds of dust
Did gather fast and thick.
The King came down from off his throne
And shook my hand in friendship true.
'Although I am the King' he said
'I cannot dance like you.'

And then the gracious Queen herself
Came slowly o'er to me.
She pinned a medal on my breast
For all the world to see,
I'll ne'er forget the words she spoke,
Or how her eyes grew dim:
'O where were you, MacAlasdair,
The day I married *him*?'

Bear Facts

It was a wonderful invitation. 'Come and shoot bear in Russia,' they cried. 'Nothing like it. Unexplored territory, seven different species of salmon rushing up the rivers, trophy sheep above the tree line, marvellous scenery – why not?'

It sounded irresistible. Small matters such as cost (boggling), hunting permits, organisation, transports and delights, all would be taken care of. All I had to do was turn up with a visa and a firearms Certificate and be wafted off in a haze of Hunter's Vodka into the far Russian yonder. And the trip was being planned for 'some time next year', which would give me a sporting chance of being able to lose some weight, break in some new boots, lose a bit more weight in case, and dream about bears.

I'd known a couple of bears as a child in Ireland. One was a wooden number, an Edwardian toy belonging to a totally gaga great-uncle who, in a rash moment of Family Feeling, had given it to me. You pulled it along by a string (it stood waist-high to me, on wheels) and it gave out the most amazing growls which set the dogs off a treat. After a week or so the dogs had become totally hysterical and the bear was banished into the attic, so that was that.

I had my own teddy bear, of course, Gladly (named after a perfectly reasonable assumption concerning the hymn 'Gladly the cross-eyed bear'), but the other bear who made a deep and powerful childhood impression was a huge stuffed thing in a cousin's house. An animal of what had undoubtedly been the most magnificent physique, it stood at the bottom of a great sweep of stairs, holding a silver salver. The trick was to climb to the top landing, three floors up, lean over the banisters and lob small stones on to the salver, which would then reverberate in the most satisfying manner. The dogs in that house weren't a model of sanity, either. In the end the poor bear, already in dire need of TLC and looking decidedly the worse for wear, got moth in its chest and had to be disposed of, together with an equally revolting elephant's-foot waste-paper bin into which I remember having been most horribly sick after a children's party.

With the prospect of coming face to face with a bear again I tried to visualise the one at the foot of the stairs: to a seven-year old child it had looked immense. Further research proved this could have been an accurate impression: it transpired that the world record bear, shot recently in the very area in which our foray was planned, stood no less than 14 feet tall, and had a front paw measurement of 13 inches across.

Now 13 inches across is a serious paw. It's bigger than your normal dinner plate. It's the size of a small gong, the hubcap on your average articulated lorry. And 14 feet tall is no sneeze either. I measured the tree outside: I can tell you, 14 foot is HIGH. More to the point for the aspiring hunter, however, is the fact that you don't have a snow-flake's chance of stopping something that size with a normal English sporting rifle – the sort of thing you might use for red deer, say.

'No problem,' they cried. 'Just nip off to one of the shoot-ing schools, they'll let you try out the right sort of rifle.'

The instructor at the shooting school was charming. He looked me up and down, made no disparaging remarks and didn't even blink at my appearance which, to be fair, must have been a tad startling: as a precaution against the recoil of a rifle which I had worked out was going to be colossal, I'd put on four of the thickest sweaters I could muster and had stuffed a pair of shooting socks, wadded into one of those soft muffin-shaped Afghan hats, into my shoulder under the jacket. I must have looked like an advertisement for weightlifters. He gently suggested that I divest myself of three of the sweaters (and, to my mortification, both the muffin hat and the socks), that I pin a recoil pad, like a wedge of jelly inside a cotton pouch, into my jacket, and give it a whirl from the bench-rest. 'I think you'll find it easier standing here. Done a bit of shooting before, have you? Well then, piece of cake.'

He was jollity personified. 'Just remember to keep your eye well back from the 'scope, can't have you bleeding all over that nice stock can we? What do you normally shoot with? Ahhhhh, wellll . . . could be a teensy bit more kick from this baby' (why DO people talk like that?) 'but not to worry, take a couple of dry shots just to get the feel of the trigger now, will you?' I leaned into the solid and comforting shape of the curved-out bench-rest and he laid the rifle – which seemed to weigh slightly more than a felled tree – into the palm of my hand and the padded glove he'd lent me, and carefully positioned the stock into my shoulder. I tried the trigger a few times, and found that I was shaking. He clamped some ear-muffs over my head and then inserted into the chamber the largest cartridge I'd ever seen, the sort of thing you'd administer to a bull elephant with piles. 'Right then, on you go, and remember to keep your cheek well down on the stock otherwise' – cheerful guffaw – 'you'll break your jaw, OK?' Right on, mate. Through the telescope sight the target seemed huge. I tried to remember about breathing, or was it not breathing, and squeezed the trigger.

When they ask you if the earth moved for you, it's never for some reason in a shooting context. All I do know is that he walked back and picked me up, adjusted the ear-muffs which were now clamped round my throat, helped me back up onto the bench-rest again, dusted me down and removed some bits of grass from my hair. 'Terrific, eh? Have another bash.'

We tried a few more times with somewhat less humiliating results – you can wedge yourself almost permanently into a bench-rest if you try hard enough – by which time my shoulder felt like pulp. It then occurred to both of us that, if I was ever actually going to shoot at a bear, it wasn't going to be propped up like this in a wooden truss. (You can't even lash yourself to a tree – it's done running backwards, or off a horse.) 'So try a free-standing shot at the target,' he suggested kindly. 'There, it's quite simple, get your feet right . . . good . . . not too heavy is it, once you get the hang of it?' He was built like a Sherman tank, so it was obviously just fine for him. He loaded the rifle and, before my knees could finally give way, I heaved it up and fired.

There was a nice story I'd read in a publication called the *Alaska Magazine* about an American explorer who had been rushed by a grizzly, and had jumped into a hole and used his back pack as protection over his head. The bear smashed the pack, then, doubtless having decided there was no more fun to be had out of that particular game, had ambled off. The surprised man heard a hissing sound, and realised that the bear's swiping paw had ignited a supply of matches in the back-pack. The ensuing fire left the explorer with third-degree burns and no jacket.

Nature red in tooth and claw was perhaps really not my scene. There was more to bears than shooting at them. Later, I thought, I would rescue Gladly from his cupboard and we'd have a quiet evening going through the Pooh books together. Meanwhile the local hospital had done sterling work and had run a nice line of stitches like a second eyebrow in what they assured me was, considering the mess, record time, and wasn't it lucky that I had an automatic gearbox as even with the sling I could still drive home one-handed?

And after all, I decided, I rather liked bears. It wasn't the perfect excuse, but it would have to do.

Fishing for Compliments

M y fishing career is not a glorious one. For years I did nothing more than throw heaps of knitting into the river at home with no success. This was always excused on the grounds that the river (Highlands and Islands variety – dour) was a spate river: so the water could always be said to be too high or too low – not clear enough or too fresh – it would be too windy or too bright, too cold or too muggy – there were a thousand good fisherman's excuses. I never spent more than half an hour trying to fling the line about, most of which would be spent disentangling it from a particularly aggressive bush, or some wires, or my ear – you know the sort of thing. I could then retire gracefully and leave the way open for someone else who knew what they were doing. The beauty of being the hostess is that you can always, if you're not desperate to do something, practise the time-honoured exercise of FHB.

The river is anyway a wonderful excuse for getting the whole house party together, in those lovely summer weeks when the friends come to stay, the house is full of all ages, and sport comes second to just having fun. Otherwise some people would be off stalking, others would be walking up snipe or rabbits, others still would be trying out bows and arrows, or writing letters, or painting, or going for long walks on the beach. But on river days, everyone came together and joined in – the ones who wanted to do nothing could do it, and read or sunbathe behind the fishing hut, you'd brought along the air rifles to shoot at cans, the bird-watchers would be blissful, the dogs were in heaven and lay round with their feet in the air. And everyone likes watching other people fish – it's very therapeutic, like watching someone else work. Picnics were always better by the water, it never mattered if the barbecue played up as there was always lots of time and no one was in a rush; and unlike at the beach, the sandwiches were sandless, and the beer and the white wine could be kept chilled under the bank.

Picnics are an art form. You get the complicated ones looking like Victorian cartoons, where the most delectable things are produced, all carefully wrought, all of which have to be kept the right way up. There should *never* have to be a right way up for anything on a picnic. Then you get the ones where the kitchen has gone into overdrive with the sandwich fillings which are over-runny and drip everywhere, so that every sandwich, as soon as it is taken out of the box, looks like a badly held bridge hand. Shooting or fishing picnics should, ideally, be kept simple. Added to which, as the hostess you have to remember that a picnic, rather like a buffet, is an institution beloved by women (who can thus be out of the pots-and-pans department) and loathed by men. Men like sitting down properly to eat, and preferably being waited on either by old butlers or young supermodels. Real men, out on sporting days, don't want to use knives and forks: they like simple things for a picnic – hare pie, ham-and-mustard doorsteps with perhaps a good dollop of fresh pâté, half a cold grouse, some decent claret or ice-cold beer, followed possibly by a bunch of Muscat grapes, a wedge of treacle tart and a hunk of cheese, preferably mousetrap. *Pace* Henley and Glyndebourne, men *really* only like picnics where they don't have to dress up for them, where it doesn't matter if something gets spilled, and where you can lie about and sleep afterwards. Someone once observed that tribes who eat sitting on the ground, wear loose clothing.

As a child I remember that my very favourite picnics were always in the car, in the rain. There is something foetal and safe, as there is in a car-wash, about watching the torrential downpour, hearing the rain thunder on the roof, being warm and cosy inside, and drinking schnapps to keep out the cold. But that was Ireland, where you were made to go swimming in winter on the grounds that it was bracing, and only did so with the bribe of cherry brandy behind the rocks afterwards. In Connemara, where we used to go for fishing holidays, the grown-ups ate and drank strange things for picnics by the lakes; pigs' trotters I remember quite clearly once, and Black Velvet, while children were palmed off with boiled eggs and fizzy drinks. I had a nanny once who made sandwiches containing dandelion leaves, but we all hated her and them with a passion and she didn't last long.

Eating on board a boat doesn't bear thinking about – all that balancing in mid-air in a Force 10, and watching which way you're facing in case you have to tear out and be sick. Sailing food is only palatable on glass-smooth turquoise seas, with the smell of freshly-caught barbecued fish wafting deliciously from the stern; or sitting in the middle of a loch with whisky and ginger biscuits while someone hauls in the trout; or in a punt with quails' eggs and champagne after Schools. I'm not – it need hardly be said – a good sailor (for years I used to think that Moby Dick was a venereal disease – I don't even read about life on the ocean wave), which is probably the secret reason why I never enjoyed fishing all that much as it, too, involves deep and unpredictable waters.

Came the moment, however, when some truly saint-like friends decided that this, this was the year when I would catch my first salmon – enough of all the ducking out of the issue; they would take me to a proper river in Scotland, where a ghillie would instruct me, and I would see just how much I loved it.

I read avidly for months beforehand, as I knew that, this time, I had to. The life and times of the salmon, its habits and proclivities; rivers and pools and how to fish them; books on how to cast, where the backswing should stop, how to tie the knots, how to stay the right way up when you fall in (NEVER WAVE is the secret, otherwise you sink like a stone; just 'Lie back in a cross formation' and scream). I read about how people wading got swept away, how many deaths were attributed annually to fishing (an amazing number) and how, if you lost your footing in a river, you should always try and float off feet first, so you wouldn't kill yourself by smashing your skull against a rock. It made riveting reading and didn't encourage me to go north and stand in a freezing fast-flowing torrent one little bit.

I then had to go off to a shop selling fishing tackle and the right sort of clothes. I'd been told not to bother with a rod, as they would lend me what I needed, but that I should definitely get the only really vital bit of equipment, namely some chest-waders. It so happened that I was returning from a wedding when I saw the shop, and was wearing a large hat with lots of veiling, a particularly pretty, rather short, silk dress, and extra-high heels. Surrounded by members of the fishing fraternity all in old frayed sweaters and tweeds, I didn't want to make too much of a meal of things so I sat down, pulled on the boot part of the waders, agreed that they fitted and bought them quickly before people started to whisper.

The first morning of the Scottish expedition we breakfasted well. It was a lovely warm day in early June and, paddling round the lodge in shooting stockings (in strange surroundings I've found that you just have to keep quiet and watch what everyone else does, it's by far the easiest way of getting it at least halfway right) I met the ghillie who was to be my mentor for the week. Small and wiry, with bow legs and a smile that would melt Jurassic rock, he appeared to take on board the fact that I'd never done it properly before, that I hadn't a clue, and please would he stick by me like glue. 'Right then,' (he spoke with an East Coast burr that sounded like a Magimix at full speed, so you only caught one sentence in four) 'ye'll come with me. Never mind all them whurrawhurrawhurrawhurra ye'll whurrawhurrawhurra fine. Grab yer boots now and we'll be off.'

I took my new waders, plus the new short fishing bum-freezer that I'd also bought, which had an inflatable collar in which you looked like a Shire horse but which was 'guaranteed to work or your money back' (comforting that – HOW?), and my old shooting hat. It's important to have something familiar with one, and I couldn't really have brought my teddy bear. We set off in his car down the road that ran alongside and above the river until we reached the beat which was ours for that day. 'Right, now you get dressed, I'll put up the rod and whurrawhurrawhurrawhurra a fish.'

I sat by the side of the road and pulled on my chest-waders. With an extra pair of thin socks on the feet, they fitted perfectly. It was only when I stood up to bring the braces up to my arms and over my shoulders and complete the dressing process in what I hoped would be a single, swift and fluid movement that I realised how stupid I'd been not to have tried it out first in the shop. But I'd had a short tight dress on then, and I'd thought that if the boot part fitted, everything would be just dandy. What I hadn't realised then, and was only just waking up to now, was that the chest-waders had been built for someone who had the same sized feet as mine but who was, clearly, some two foot shorter in height. The braces, at full stretch and twanging, came up to just below tit level, and the crotch was between my knees.

It was not an auspicious beginning. You can't say to a sixty-five-year-old ghillie, whom you've just met for the first time, a man of the utmost probity and probably an Elder of the Church of Scotland, 'Hey I'm sorry, I'll just have to fish in my tights and my best lace knickers and the short dinky bumfreezer so kindly excuse my *derrière* and which fly do you suggest using to start off with, my man?'

He might take it as a professional foul. So, hoping that he hadn't noticed (he was at that moment anyway deeply ensconced in his fly boxes and performing knots and twirls like a dervish), I undid the braces, rolled the top of the waders down a bit, tied the braces round my waist in a granny-knot and shuffled over, casually, to join him.

When you are trying to walk in a pair of trousers (or

chest-waders) of which the crotch is at knee level, it's like trying to do the can-can with a steel vice around your knees. You can't. You're hobbled. All movement of the legs upwards is impossible, your knees are clamped together and the only thing you can manage is a waddle like a duck, feet well apart for some semblance of balance. Or bunny-hop, as in a sack race. This looks pretty stupid on a river bank, and the only barely redeeming feature of the situation was that he was in front, carrying the rod, his little bow legs going like the clappers, keeping up a steady stream of 'whurrawhurrawhurra' which I was too busy bunny-hopping to catch. I did notice though that, on the high road above the river, various cars were slowing down, some even coming to a halt, to watch this amazing progression of The Ghillie and His Rod down by the water's edge; but all I could do was carry on, pretending that nothing was amiss, and praying that I could break my ankle on a boulder and be able to lie down and be carried home so that no one would ever know.

Worse was, of course, to follow. It was fine once we'd come to a halt and started to fish, as you can shuffle slowly into the water over a bit of shingle and it looks as if you mean it. But twenty minutes later, at the bottom of the pool ('Now don't be taking big steps, just a wee bitty at a time like' – big steps? The circulation was beginning to go from the knees up, and I only hoped I wasn't going to have to leap like Jeremy Fisher from one rock to another as I'd have been a goner), you had to clamber out and up the bank where it had become steep. And being unable to separate one knee from another makes the action of clambering up a 4-foot bank a total no-no. Having handed him the rod, I would wait until he'd turned away and was whurra-whurrawhurra-ing off again to a new spot downstream, hurl myself bodily at the bank, landing on my stomach, then thrash and wiggle up on to my knees, by now numb and devoid of all sensation. It was hell.

This went on all morning. It was worse than doing skiing exercises in a garbage bag. I was sweating like a pig and starting to shake and the only really miraculous thing was that no fish ever came near me as I knew that, totally lacking any real form of balance, if I'd ever managed to get in to one, at the first tug on the line I'd have been face down after it, no feet-first nonsense either, and out into the wide Sargasso Sea or wherever the blazes we were. I kept on looking longingly at my watch, but no help came from there either.

Finally, rescue was at hand. There was a shout from the road. Friends had come to see how we were getting on, armed with rugs and picnic basket and a fish-bag in case . . . And, as the ghillie and I emerged from the water and I handed him the rod as usual, and hurled myself once more onto the waist-high bank to perform the usual floundering gyrations, thrashing about on the grass and the thistles like some large green sheep, I heard the sound of someone snorting. The ghillie had turned, and finally seen me.

I've never seen someone laugh like that. He laughed until he went puce. He choked, and held his sides, and sat down on the grass, and wept. And the friends, making their way down towards us, saw what was going on and hurried over, and joined in until the tears ran down their faces. 'Well Willy, landed a big one there,' one of them managed to gulp out before subsiding into hysteria again.

I cut my way out of the bloody things, wrapped myself in a rug, and we had the very best picnic I can ever recall. I don't actually remember what we ate, but there was an awful lot of gin and tonic to wash it down with and I don't drink gin. Normally. That afternoon I was driven, stupefied, to the local stores where a pair of decent simple thigh waders was produced, and money changed hands. I don't remember anything of the drive back.

And I never caught a fish all week, either.

A Palpable Hit

I started shooting at Bisley by accident. I'd been there on all of four occasions, lured by a nice invitation to 'bring a picnic and have a look at the place, I've got a bit of practising to do, you could fire a shot or two if you like, it's a lovely day,' by a friend of my husband's who was a noted shot and who had originally taught me to shoot with a .22 out of the gun room window in Scotland. We drove down, we picnicked, he shot, he let me fire a few rounds, we left. Next week, same thing – but this time I fired at a target 1100 yards away, which seemed incredible. Then we picnicked, he shot and we left. Same thing the two following weeks, only each time, he made me shoot a little more.

As we drove back to London after the fourth excursion, he timed it beautifully. We were batting along the M3, and I couldn't jump out. 'By the way,' he said breezily, 'next week there are the annual Match Rifle competitions, the Imperial Meeting. And you're entered.' He had filled in the forms, my husband had forged my signature, he had a rifle I could use and that was that. The newspapers subsequently referred to it as 'She was entered without her knowledge', which I thought was a bit off, really.

My mother was totally appalled. 'DARLING you can't, Bisley, I mean, all those MEN, it's so unladylike, what WOULD your grandmother have said?' My grandmother, long since dead and the epitome of Edwardian elegance, who in her youth had won many a fine silver snuffbox for her prowess at archery and who had also been a lovely shot over the snipe bogs, would, I felt, have approved unequivocally. My father, who had served with Glubb in the desert, thought it was a perfectly splendid idea. Bisley was, after all, a well-known range used by the military where old *old* Lord Cottesloe had put up a pair of blackgame in 1890 . . . 'Why not? Brutal and licentious soldiery though, hmmm? Better take a hatpin.'

My mother turned my picture to the wall. I set forth one hot day in early July for my first Imperial Meeting at Bisley, stopping just short of the National Rifle Association gates to throw up in a hedge.

That first Meeting was amazing, like entering a time-warp where nothing much had changed for a hundred years; each subsequent year it was just as extraordinary, just as nerve-racking, but somehow, as you became more familiar with the place so you noticed change, care, new paint, old buildings lovingly restored, bright colours, flags everywhere like some latter-day Camelot. There are tents and striped Victorian pavilions, barracks and clubhouses, caravans, lodges and huts; weather-vanes, barge-boards and gables with twiddly bits; corrugated roofs and tiny,

immaculate, brightly painted ticket-boxes, like bathing huts, on wheels. And an old train sitting in a petticoat of buttercups. Tubs of flowers stand in front of smart brick or wooden buildings, roses smother walls, gorse and heather rampage by the pine woods out beyond the ranges and the old tall square clocktower, its roof picked out in blue and yellow, stands like a beacon at the hub of this wild and unspoiled countryside.

And each year, each Imperial Meeting, a cast of thousands. Schoolboys and girls tumble out of vans, soldiers move at the double. Every country of the world seems to be represented: Canadian and German, South African and Jamaican, French and Irish, Zambian and Scot. There are people in uniform with medals, people in shorts with sunburn, people in shooting jackets with mackintosh trousers, people in camouflage, people in jeans. They mill around scoreboards, stride about carrying rifles, gossip in doorways or drink under hanging baskets on verandah steps. Bands play under the chestnut trees, radios blare under sleeping-tents, medical staff tend to those under the weather. There are children and dogs, clerics and commodores; there are are ice-cream vendors and hot-dog stalls. Girls sell souvenirs, officials chat to walkie talkies; immaculate old men in blazers with beribboned lapels saunter over lawns, women take tea in wicker chairs, boys struggle with guyropes, patient Griseldas hang out washing in the caravan lines. There is a vast room filled with silver trophies. There are vehicles of every shape and age, vans and cars, old Daimlers and mopeds, army trucks and wheelchairs, bicycles and water-carts. And everyone wears a hat.

Wandering into clubhouses, offices or private huts, seeing the rows upon rows of medals, names and records, the old prints, the sepia photographs of wonderfully ancient figures in canvas baths and beards – soldier servants in attendance – you are struck by the sheer arcane magic of the place. In those early days of Bisley, the late 1800s, it was very formalised, very regimented, restricted in both format and style, Edwardian and proper, women out of camp by ten p.m., and most of the men stood well away from the razor. Nowadays, it is the variety that is remarkable – both in denizens as in disciplines. In the old days, shooting was only geared towards men, perfecting skill-at-arms; now shooting is a sport, not a duty, and whether you are male or female (there is no distinction in shooting competitions between the sexes) you can do any form of shooting that takes your fancy. Lorryloads of military still run up and down battering Falling Plates, but now there are Grouse Drives and High Pheasants for shotgun enthusiasts up in the wood, as well as the skeet layout and Down the Line; airgunners ping away at small targets on posts in the undergrowth; sporting men in tweeds shoot the Running Deer, and black-powder zealots crouch under vast umbrellas and clouds of smoke. You can shoot at every distance between 6 and 1200 yards with every type of pistol, rifle or shotgun ever invented, either on indoor ranges or out over the great fields where the huge blue-and-yellow wind-flags fly. The decibel level is astonishing. Then the hooter goes, and everything stops for lunch.

When I first came to Bisley, having only done a bit of stalking – an atavistic, comparatively solitary sport on remote and peaceful hills – I hadn't a clue about competitive shooting or the Match Rifle discipline of the longer ranges into which I had been propelled, or the formalities and rituals of the thing. But everyone was terribly kind. Charming gentlemen enquired solicitously of one's progress, undergraduates in ice-cream jackets offered to carry one's rifle, wives and other female shots offered tea, sympathy and aspirin.

They all went out of their way to steer me through that first complicated week. If you shot badly, they commiserated;

if you did well, they had an engaging way of rushing up after and enthusing and making you feel simply brilliant – the elephant herd, making sure the newcomer is all right.

And it's a very gentlemanly sport. There's no gamesmanship, no bitching. People raise their hats to bid you good morning, and don't go round kicking the cat when it all goes wrong. And when it does go wrong, and you've made a real horlicks and you hope no one has noticed (they all do of course, it's up on the stats board in a matter of minutes) they say NOT to worry, it really was an impossible wind, no one made much of it, there's always tomorrow, after all.

Shooters do it on a shooting mat, according to the stickers: you have to learn the terminology. It takes a little time and, at the beginning, there are certain expressions which to the innocent lady novice can be a trifle startling. There are things like 'blowing off' – apparently a perfectly seemly thing to do even in mixed company – or tightening up your bedding screws, or even getting things stuck in your chamber, which *did* sound painful. But you quickly learn to nod sagely and silently and find out later about these extraordinary occurences. 'Unusually large rise I had there,' confided one old boy as we stepped off the firing-point after a particularly difficult shoot, 'always happens on a cold day.' No one even blinked.

Quickly, you get the hang of it. You lie down at, say, 1000 yards for your 15- or 20-shot shoot. You make sure your ear-muffs fit properly and that you have everything you need. Like the bolt in the rifle, and enough ammunition. (It does happen.) The voice booms over the loudspeaker 'Ladies and gentlemen, you may commence firing when your target appears,' and then I panic, as I can't remember which target I'm on. Ninety-nine other people on either side start shooting in pairs, you concentrate like mad on the wind-flags, write down your partner's score (he's on your right, so he goes first), look through the spotting 'scope to check the target, adjust the wind-gauge on your rifle, try and let off a good shot and not wobble, pray you've got it right and wait for the target to come up with your scoring panel on it; curse yourself for being so stupid, write down your score and the position of the orange spotting-disc on the target which indicates where your shot went, while your partner fires his next shot . . . and so on for forty minutes or so, perhaps three or four times a day.

But precisely because it's so daft – because you're trying to hit the centre of a small black blob in the middle of a white target at what seems like an unconscionable distance; because every single shot is different; because every merest wisp of wind, or the air temperature, can affect the bullet and send it careering away from your point of aim; because it requires total concentration, total oblivion to everything and everyone else, it becomes addictive. Every time a bullseye is signalled, you just want to get on and do it again. And if it's not a bullseye this shot, then maybe the next one will be. Or the next . . .

If you shoot Olympic disciplines, if you're invited to join a team and shoot for your country, then it becomes more serious and you do exercises and get fit and go in for team psychology. But if you simply shoot as an individual and for fun, as often or as little as you want, then it becomes a totally exhilarating sport. You can be as old as God (and lots of them are) or a novice, you can come from any conceivable walk of life, and you will still be shooting only against yourself in a bid for perfection which ultimately only you can achieve. All that matters is your own effort, trying to produce your own personal best.

They call it the triumph of hope over experience. I've shot at Bisley now for more years than I care to remember: I still throw up in the hedge before every Imperial Meeting, and it's probably the week I most look forward to in the whole year.